SMITHSONIAN HISTORY OF WARFARE

WARS OF THE
ANCIENT GREEKS

WARS OF THE ANCIENT GREEKS

VICTOR DAVIS HANSON

JOHN KEEGAN, SERIES EDITOR

Smithsonian Books

Collins

An Imprint of HarperCollins*Publishers*

For W. K. Pritchett, who revolutionized the study of Ancient Greek warfare

Text © 1999 by Victor Davis Hanson
Design and layout © 1999 by Cassell & Co.
First published in Great Britain 1999
The picture credits on page 240 constitute an extension to this copyright page.

Material in the introduction and chapter 5 is based on ideas that appeared in Victor Davis Hanson and John Heath, *Who Killed Homer? The Demise of Classical Education and the Recovery of Greek Wisdom* (The Free Press, New York, 1998) and Victor Davis Hanson, "Alexander the Killer," *Quarterly Journal of Military History,* spring 1998, 10.3, 8–20.

Published 2004 in the United States of America by Smithsonian Books
In association with Cassell
Wellington House, 125 Strand
London WC2R 0BB

Library of Congress Cataloging-in-Publication data
Hanson, Victor Davis.
    Wars of the ancient Greeks / Victor Davis Hanson ; John Keegan, general editor.
      p.   cm.— (Smithsonian history of warfare)
    Includes bibliographical references and index.
    ISBN-13: 978-0-06-114208-6.
    1. Greece—History, Military—To 146 BC. I. Keegan, John, 1934– II. Title. III.
Series.

DF89.H36   2004
355'.00938—dc22   2004049101

Manufactured in China, not at government expense
09 08   2 3 4 5

Title page: Gold Quiver from Royal Tomb of King Philip II of Macedonia from Verghina 350–340 BC. Detail of warriors fighting. Archaeological Museum, Salonika.

Overleaf: Until the early fifth century when this black-figure vase was painted, in theory hoplites wore the full panoply of bronze breastplate, greaves, and Corinthian helmet and on occasion carried two thrusting spears. Hoplite spearmen dominate black-figure vase-painting, whereas bowmen, skirmishers, and foreigners are less prominent and without heroic idealization.

Front cover: Vase painting. Photo: Bridgeman Art Library.

Back cover: Roman floor mosaic portrays Alexander (left) in the battle of Issus (333). Photo: Peter Newark Pictures. Map: Arcadia Editions.

Acknowledgments

I would like to thank John Keegan and Judith Flanders for asking me to write this volume on the Ancient Greeks at war. My colleague at California State University, Fresno, Professor Bruce Thornton, kindly read the book in manuscript and offered his usual perceptive suggestions. Penny Gardiner superbly supervised the difficult task of turning a rough manuscript into an illustrated book.

All dates are BC unless otherwise noted; I have retained those Latinized forms of Greek nouns that are more familiar to a general audience.

I owe an enormous debt of gratitude, as do all students of Ancient Greek history, to W. K. Pritchett, whose five volumes on the Greek state at war, and eight companion books on Greek topography, have prompted a renaissance in the study of Classical warfare.

Victor Davis Hanson
Selma, California
October 1997

Contents

KEY TO MAPS

General symbols

 site of battle

 fort or fortified settlement

 movement

Geographical symbols

 urban area

urban area (3D maps)

river

seasonal river

canal

• town/city

internal border

international border

Map list

A Millennium of Greek Wars

1250	Traditional date of the Trojan war
1200	End of Mycenaean civilization
1100–800	'Dark Ages' in Greece
725–675	Composition of the Homeric poems
730–660	Spartan defeat of Messenia; enslavement of helots
750–650	Rise of the Greek city state; appearance of hoplites
700	Lelantine war between Chalcis and Eretria
669	Spartan defeat by Argos at Hysiae
560	Battle of the Fetters; Tegea defeats Sparta
550	Battle of the Champions; Sparta defeats Argos
507	Creation of democracy at Athens
499–494	Revolts of Ionians against Persia
494	Sparta obliterates the Argives at Sepeia
490	First Persian war, battle of Marathon
480	Invasion of Xerxes, battles of Thermopylae and Salamis
479	Conclusion of Persian wars, battles of Plataea and Mycale
479–431	Great fifty years of Athenian maritime supremacy
471	Sparta defeats Arcadians at Dipaea
457	Athenian defeat at Tanagra, but subsequent victory the same year over the Boeotians at Oenophyta
447	Boeotians defeat Athenians at first battle of Coronea
440	Successful Athenian siege of island of Samos
431	Outbreak of Peloponnesian war
431–425	Peloponnesian invasions of Attica
429	Death of Pericles
425	Spartan débâcle at Pylos and Sphacteria
424	Battle between Thebans and Athenians at Delium
418	Spartan victory at first Mantinea
415–413	Athenian expedition to Sicily
415–404	Spartan garrison at Decelea

405	Athenian naval defeat at Aegospotami
404	End of Peloponnesian war and defeat of Athens
401–400	March of Xenophon and the Ten Thousand
399	Artillery first used on Sicily
396–395	Spartan king Agesilaus in Asia Minor
395	Death of Lysander at Haliartus
394	Spartan victories at Nemea and Coronea
390	Destruction of Spartan regiment near Corinth
375	Theban defeat of Sparta at Tegyra
371	Spartan defeat by Epaminondas at Leuctra
370	Epaminondas' first invasion of Sparta, founding of Messene
362	Theban–Spartan standoff at second battle of Mantinea
339	Victory of Timoleon over the Carthaginians in Sicily
338	Defeat of allied Greeks at Chaeronea by Philip II
336	Death of Philip; ascension of Alexander
335	Thebes destroyed by Alexander
334–323	Campaigns of Alexander the Great in Asia
334	Battle at the Granicus
333	Battle of Issus
331	Battle of Gaugamela
326	Battle at the Hydaspes
323	Death of Alexander the Great
323–281	Wars of the Diadochi (Alexander's Successors)
301	Defeat of Antigonus at Ipsus
280–279	Pyrrhus' invasion of Italy
217	Ptolemy defeats Antiochus III at Raphia
197	Roman victory over Macedonians at Cynoscephalae
189	Roman final defeat over Antiochus III at Magnesia
168	Defeat of Macedonians by Romans at Pydna
146	Sack of Corinth, final Roman conquest of Greece

The Greek Military Legacy

To the Greeks war and peace, spear and staff, and soldier and sage were complementary, never antithetical. Here, a hoplite with fearsome designs on his shield and shield apron receives advice from an aged learned man in robes. Aeschylus, Demosthenes and Socrates at various times were dressed similarly to both figures on this Attic red-figure pot.

The Greek military legacy

'ALWAYS EXISTING BY NATURE between every Greek city state', so Plato said of war. Most Greeks agreed: war was about the most important thing we humans do. It was fighting – not philosophy, not literature, not architecture, not vase-painting – that best revealed virtue, cowardice, skill or ineptitude, civilization or barbarism. For his own epitaph the dramatist Aeschylus wrote of his one-day experience at Marathon – with not a mention of his authorship of the monumental trilogy, the *Oresteia*.

War and the use of land are the building blocks of Aristotle's *Politics* and Plato's *Republic*. Both utopias assume that before man can speculate, contemplate, educate and argue, he must first figure out how to eat and how to fight. The soldier and the farmer may be forgotten or even despised in our own culture, but in the Greek mind agriculture and warfare were central to a workable society, in which both professions were to be controlled by a rational and egalitarian citizenry. There is not a major Greek figure of the fifth century – intellectual, literary, political – who did not either own a farm or fight. Very often he did both.

Pericles

War –'the father of all, the king of all', the philosopher Heraclitus says – for good or evil is innate to human kind and thus nearly the central topic of all Greek literature. The Trojan war was not Homer's alone; murderous Achilles, stubborn Ajax and sneaky Odysseus, warriors all, form the backdrop of the very best of Classical Greek tragedy. Aristophanes' comedies, from the *Acharnians* to the *Lysistrata*, make burlesque nonsense out of the senselessness of the Peloponnesian war. The lyrics and elegies of the poets Archilochus, Callinus, Alcaeus, even Sappho would be lost without hoplite shields, bronze armour, an armada of ships, and Lydian chariots. Most Greek gods – Zeus, Athena, Poseidon, Artemis, Ares – were portrayed in either song or art as warriors, who as outsized hoplites killed or shielded mortals on the battlefield. Few, if any, cultures have been so steeped in war as the Classical city states without becoming as little militarized.

Plato's stepfather, Pericles' son and Aeschylus' brother were wounded or killed as a result of battle. Melissus, the Samian philosopher and student of Parmenides, led his fleet into battle against Pericles himself, both intellectuals knowing something of oarsmanship and ramming. Sophocles was somewhere at sea nearby, as part of the elected high command of Athenians who came to enslave the island of Samos. Greek generals were often noted historians and poets – Thucydides, Xenophon and

Sophocles

Tyrtaeus come quickly to mind. The great mathematician Archimedes died in the siege of Syracuse, in his last days crafting military machines against the Romans.

Nearly every Greek temple has its friezes and pediments full of gods sculpted in the hoplite battledress of the *polis*; vase-painting glorifies the ranks of the phalanx; grave steles portray the deceased in infantry armour. Plato often uses the paradigm of war to illustrate his theories of virtue and knowledge, his examples often drawn from the personal experience of the middle-aged Socrates fighting at the battles of Amphipolis, Delium and Potidaea. There is not a single Greek historian whose main theme is not war. For Herodotus, Thucydides or Xenophon to write historical narratives of anything else was apparently inconceivable. Heraclitus said, 'Souls killed in war are purer than those who die of diseases.' The poets Mimnermus, Callinus and Simonides agreed. For Socrates, founder of western philosophy, killing men in battle for Athens was not in conflict with the practice of abstract inquiry and dialectics, and Kant's idea of a perpetual peace was neither envisioned nor sought after by the Greeks.

The Greek legacy, then, is more than rationalism, empiricism, capitalism or consensual government. The Greeks created a unique approach to organized fighting that within a century proved to be the most lethal brand of warfare in the Mediterranean, the chief tenets of which have characterized western military tradition ever since. As our century ends the world is moving toward western political ideals with ever increasing speed: market capitalism, democratization, individualism, private property, free trade and fluid foreign investment are now acknowledged as the global culture, as the only systems of economic organization and political culture that seem more or less to work.

Ultimately the protection of that political and economic agenda depends on a unique practice of arms. After the Second World War and the end of the Cold War there now seems only one way to fight – but this legacy goes back to the *polis* Greeks and no further. At the millennium almost all military technology is either purchased from western powers – America, Europe, the UK, or the westernized East such as Japan and Korea – or engineered and fabricated on western designs. Military education and doctrine – everything from the organization of divisions, brigades and companies, to the ranking of generals, colonels and majors – is western inspired.

Western armies are free of religious fanaticism and subject to civilian control and audit. Their soldiers, like Greek hoplites of old, are not shanghaied into service, but enter the armed forces with understood rights and responsibilities, the violation of which is subject to trial and appeal, not a firing squad. In short, western military forces are composed of better trained and disciplined troops, which are better equipped and led by better generals than any others in the world today.

Even the most virulently anti-western nations concede this. Only through the emulation of western arms can they ensure a chance of survival in an increasingly unsafe and unpredictable world of guided

Socrates

missiles and laser-directed shells. If, at the end of this millennium, we still see military cabals, warrior clans, ambush, skirmish, primitive weaponry and hit-and-run liberation fighters on our universal television screens, it is by default, not choice. Those belligerents lack the technology, the organization, the education and the capital to meet their opponents face-to-face in a cruel and near-instantaneous decision with sophisticated arms, logistics and transportation. Indeed, even the occasional success of irregulars depends entirely on their access to western-designed arms – grenade-launchers, hand-held missiles and land-mines.

In sum, western warfare is terrifying – both relatively and absolutely. The march of European armies has been both reckless and murderous, ultimately smashing anything that has raised its head in over two millennia of organized military opposition. Other belligerent traditions in China, the Americas, India and the Pacific islands also boast a continuous military culture of great duration. But they cannot claim a practice of similar effectiveness and flexibility, or a warring capability so accomplished in its devastation, as Alexander's decade-long swath to the Ganges, Caesar's 'pacification' of Gaul, the six-year spoliation of

Europe in the Second World War, or the single-day atomization of Hiroshima and Nagasaki attest.

So utterly deadly has this Greek-inspired western warfare become that in the last decade of the twentieth century it has nearly put itself out of business: the collision of national armies in Europe, the decisive exchange between nuclear powers (the ultimate spectre of western military technology) will lead now not to political resolution and peace but only to barbarism and extinction. If today mere embargo, sanction and counter-insurgency suffice to combat the terrorist and the thug, it is also because the age-old western solution to such challenges – a brutal and quick resolution through massive firepower – is worse medicine than the disease, raising the ante for its squabbling players to abject annihilation.

This admission of the clear fighting superiority of the West must not be interpreted as mere Eurocentrism. Great evil has also been wrought by the efficacy of occidental military doctrine. Indigenous gallant peoples in the Americas and Africa have been slaughtered for no good purpose by the callous skill of Europeanized forces. Alexander sought no 'Brotherhood of Man' in Asia. His ten-year legacy is more accurately seen as a decade of carnage, rape, pillage and arson that left feuding and megalomaniac brawlers, not nation-builders, in its immediate wake.

The tens of millions that were slain in the First and Second World Wars must also in some sense be seen as a logical culmination of the ferocious military tradition of the Greeks that in the last two centuries has once again turned its penultimate destructiveness on its own, at the Somme, at Verdun, at Normandy and at Dresden. Indeed, the organization, efficiency, and systematic carnage of the death camps in Germany and eastern Europe of half a century ago are perhaps best understandable as vile and aberrant appendages of

Alexander

18

western militarism itself. With Hitler, Mussolini and Treblinka in mind, it is better to see the martial efficacy of the West as relentless and driving, rather than predictably good or evil.

What makes western arms so accomplished – and so horrific on the battlefield – is a series of practices created at the beginning of western culture by the Greeks. Yet this military legacy, so fundamental to the expansion and survival of the later West, is today often forgotten at its moment of greatest triumph. Books on 'the legacy of the Greeks' and 'the western tradition' cover everything from science to architecture, but rarely, if ever, mention warfare, despite this being the central experience of Classical Greece.

To respond to that neglect, the following chapters discuss recurring themes – social, economic, political, religious, moral – that form the substructure of Greek military practice. These larger issues explain why Greek warfare was so relentless and so virulent, and reveal its role – both positive and pernicious – in Classical culture. The obvious aim is to see in ancient warfare ancient culture itself; to inquire why, at the end of the present millennium, the military traditions of Greece alone seem to predominate, offering both comfort and peril for all who would claim their heritage.

But what is this abstraction, 'the Greek way of war', which has provided the core of our later western military tradition? It is not superior courage. All cultures produce gallant men. King Xerxes' Immortals who charged King Leonidas and his Spartans at Thermopylae were brave fighters. So were the fierce Thracians who so perplexed Philip's Macedonian phalangites. Herodotus' history is often a paean to the battle gallantry of non-Greeks. Nor did the Greeks invent the military ethos. Long before the creation of Classical Sparta, Near Eastern and Egyptian societies boasted of élite bodies of chariot warriors, whose profession was to fight, kill, and die bravely for their theocratic dynasts. Indeed, other than in Sparta, the Greeks were never much of a militarized society, despite Max Weber's portrait of a supposed *kriegerisches Volk*.

This modern bronze statue of the Spartan king and general Leonidas stands not far from the spot where Leonidas and his 299 followers were killed to the last man by the Persians at Thermopylae. Leonidas vowed to hold the pass or die, and delayed the Persian advance for enough time to give his coalition army of more than 7,000 a chance to retreat in safety and warn the other Greeks.

The idea of large armies owes nothing to the Greeks either. During the entire history of the city state, the Greeks were usually outnumbered by Persians, Egyptians, Medes, Gauls, and just about every other culture with which they collided. Both western European tribes and eastern centralized palatial cultures were far more successful than the Greeks at rallying enormous hordes of fighting men.

How, then, did the city states create a military paradigm so adroit at conquering such enemies, when the Greeks had no premium either on battle courage, or militarism – or even the ability to bring superior numbers of combatants to the battlefield? Are not battles mostly won by fielding the greatest number of brave men?

Rarely, if at all. Rather, the Greek way of war encompasses a few core values distilled from the larger cultural, political and economic practices of the city state at large. Greek warfare is only an extension of Greek society, and thus, just as philosophy, democracy, personal freedom, citizenship and free expression are ideas found nowhere else in the Mediterranean, so too the military corollaries of such values are equally singular – and nearly as matchless in achieving the goals for which they are designed.

The military mastery of the Greeks can be summarized broadly by eight general military customs and beliefs which are unique to the Hellenic and indeed later European tradition, and which remain thematic throughout the four-century life of the city state (700–300):

1. **Advanced technology:** the unsurpassed excellence of both weapons and armour, a superiority in design and craftsmanship over non-Greek equipment that was wide-ranging and well-established, from the hoplite breastplate and shield to the Macedonian sarissa, from catapults to wheeled siege engines – all novel designs and fabrications that brought their creators money and fame, rarely exile, execution or loss of freedom.

2. **Superior discipline:** the effective training and ready acceptance of command by soldiers themselves, whether in the close-knit ranks of the Classical phalanx or the ad hoc democratic councils of the mercenary Ten Thousand stuck in Persia. The laws of good battle order flowed from the consensus of the Assembly; thus adherence to such discipline was simply a ratification of prior individual expression and group concord.

3. **Ingenuity in response:** an intellectual tradition, unfettered and uncensored by either government or religion, that sought constant improvement in the face of challenge. That market-place of ideas explains why under duress Greeks figured out first how to counter elephants and then how to incorporate them into their own armies; why the Near Eastern practice of siegecraft in Greek hands became the science of obliterating, not of merely taking cities; why within a decade Athens had not only created a fleet from nothing, but had essentially destroyed the Persian armada at Salamis. No Greek felt ashamed or

unsure about adopting, modifying, rejecting – or improving – military practices that were originally not his own.

4. The creation of a broad, shared military observance among the majority of the population: the preference for citizen militias and civilian participation in military decision-making, that led, as Aristotle saw it, to a clear battlefield edge over mercenaries. A quarter of a million Persian subjects and mercenaries were assembled at the battle of Plataea under duress; about half that number of Greeks mustered willingly, subservient only to the majority will of their assemblies. At Plataea, the former fought well, the latter fought possessed. The idea of an entire free citizenry in arms is entirely Hellenic.

5. Choice of decisive engagement: the preference to meet the enemy head-on, hand-to-hand in shock battle, and to resolve the fighting as quickly and decisively as possible, battle being simply the final military expression of the majority will of the citizenry. The Persians felt a destructive madness had come upon the Greeks at Marathon, and so it had, as they ran head-on into the Persian ranks, a practice frightening to behold for the easterner, as the battles at Plataea, Cunaxa, Granicus, Issus and Gaugamela attest.

6. Dominance of infantry: the notion that property-owners on foot with muscular strength, not horsemen or even missile-men, alone win wars. Ultimately, what destroyed non-Greek armies – and what shredded the ranks of other Hellenic armies – were hoplites and phalangites, who alone could march forward, clear the way ahead, and then possess the ground they stood upon. Citizens who have title to their own farms, live on that ground, and can pass on that investment to their children, inevitably wish to obtain and hold land – and will not easily give it up.

7. A systematic application of capital to warmaking: the ability to collect assessments, impose tribute and borrow monies to field men and matériel for extensive periods of time. Athens fought well and long because it knew how to raise the necessary money to hire, purchase, rent and borrow men and matériel long after it should have been defeated by a host of more numerous enemies. Alexander could go east because an entire cadre of astute treasurers knew how to tax and steal, and then mint that largess to pay for a sophisticated quartermaster corps – over 1,000 tons of food, water and forage were supplied to Alexander's army for every day it marched.

8. A moral opposition to militarism: the ubiquity of literary, religious, political and artistic groups who freely demanded justification and explication of war, and thus often questioned and occasionally arrested the unwise application of military force. The Trojan war, the conflict between Sparta and Athens, and Alexander's murderous rampage through Asia are all the subject of a hostile literature. That Greek warmakers were to be the stuff of artistic, literary and religious criticism resulted in a questioning of aims and procedures – an ongoing debate that ironically often refined and ratified rather than simply hindered Hellenic attack.

The Greek way of war should not be an encomium to the contemporary western efficacy of killing large numbers of people. Western warfare starts out with the Classical Greeks as an ethical practice to preserve society; but its very allegiance to the free economic and political expression of the individual creates a dynamism that without care can lead to the destruction of western culture itself. If anything, these chapters should reveal this dual legacy of the Greeks. The story of Hellenic arms is but a constant see-saw struggle between the Greek genius for applying economic and political prowess to the battlefield, and the effort to harness the lethal result within a framework of largely ethical, legal and moral considerations – a dilemma that began with the Greeks, but whose solution we in the West have yet to solve.

CHAPTER ONE

Early Greek Fighting (1400–750)

The Lion Gate – *the heads of the matched pair of guardian regal lionesses were missing when excavators uncovered the entryway – marked the grand access way to the palace of Mycenae itself. These so-called 'Cyclopean' walls were thicker and sometimes even higher than fortifications during Classical times; their construction (1350–1300) may have taken many generations and reflects a degree of political regimentation and coercion impossible during the era of the city state. The lintel below the lionesses is 15 feet long, nearly 7 feet thick, and over 3 feet high at its centre; it may have weighed 20 tons. Two massive doors over 10 feet high barred entry. Attackers had their unshielded right arms exposed to a guard tower that commanded the approaches to the gateway on the right, while a fortification wall to the left ensured a steady rain of missiles from the palace's defenders.*

Palace war as evolutionary dead end: the collapse of Mycenaean Greece

CULTURE AND CIVILIZATION EXISTED on the Greek mainland long before the city state (700–300). Earlier Mycenaeans (1600–1100) spoke almost the same Hellenic language as their Greek successors. Their gods were more or less the same Olympians. The distant memory of Mycenaean kings and generals, citadels and burial vaults provided the historical kernel to later Greek myth-making and epic. Many Mycenaean palace-sites were resettled by Greeks during the Dark Ages (1100–800) and the Archaic Period (700–500), proving a continuity of Greek occupation, unbroken from the second millennium to the Roman annexation.

The citadel of Mycenae occupied a natural atoll amid the rich farmland of the northern Argolid. Unlike the acropolis of the later city state, the Mycenaean fortified palace was the central residence and administrative centre of a royal élite, which collected, stored and redistributed harvests from the surrounding plain.

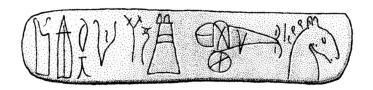

Linear B was the script of the Mycenaean citadels and discovered on baked clay tablets at Mycenae, Tiryns, Pylos, Thebes and Cnossus. Most tablets date from the thirteenth century and were used to record inventories and administrative decrees of an imperial élite. This particular tablet from the Mycenaean palace at Cnossus on Crete apparently records the issue of body armour, horse and chariot from the palace storehouses.

But there all similarity ceases. The Mycenaeans' written language of record-keeping, Linear B, their political, social and economic organization, together with their values, were not passed on to the Greeks of the historical period. It comes as no surprise that the practice of Mycenaean warfare – itself almost Near Eastern in tradition – ended also with the sudden collapse of the palaces in Greece.

Until nearly 1200 Mycenaean warmaking was probably not very different from the fighting that had been practised for centuries to the east and south in the Mediterranean by the Egyptians and Hittites: onslaughts of light-armed skirmishers and missile-men clustering around chariots equipped with well-armoured javelin-throwers and bowmen. From the Linear B tablet inventories, a few painted remains on vases, the finds of metallic armour and weapons, and Mycenaean memories in later Greek literature, we should imagine that the lord, or wanax, of local sovereignties at Mycenae, Tiryns, Argos, Pylos, Thebes, Gla, Orchomenos and Athens directed political, economic and military affairs from fortified citadels – palaces guarded by walls ranging from 10 to 30 feet in thickness and sometimes over 25 feet in height. Yet the circuits were usually quite small and never encompassed much more than dynastic residences and palace stores. Such massive fortifications – the remains of the walls were imagined by later perplexed Greeks to be the work of earlier superhumans and thus called Cyclopean – reveal the

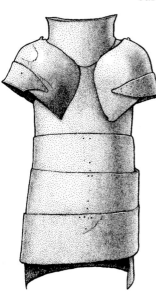

core values of Mycenaean palatial culture. Material and human capital were invested in protecting – and often burying – scribes, bureaucrats and royalty, rather than in fielding large armies of infantrymen to protect surrounding farmlands and general population through pitched battles. Later Classical Greek walls are not so thick, but encompass far greater territory – revealing the emphases of the respective cultures.

In the same way that land was allotted by the Mycenaean wanax to various segments of the population, and in turn harvests were brought back to Mycenaean palaces for storage and redistribution, so too the written records of the Linear B inventories suggest that the king and his chief military commander controlled the fabrication and stockpiling of weaponry and the mobilization of his subjects. Before 1300 bronze armour and weaponry were rigid and cumbersome, which suggests that the Mycenaean chariots were deployed almost like modern tanks, platforms for the discharge of missiles and arrows. These vehicles were used to run over and break through foot soldiers, and to serve as islands of protection for accompanying swarms of lightly clad skirmishers to enter and exit the fray. Chariot-drivers, archers, and missile troops, who were deployed in

The so-called Dendra Cuirass dates from the fifteenth century and most probably belonged to one of a small cadre of wealthy charioteers, since the concentric circles of bronze would have made walking or even bending nearly impossible. The helmet was crafted from boars' teeth, and is mentioned by Homer. It also appears on early frescos from Thera.

and about the citadel fortifications, were specialized warriors rather than part of a large militia.

By the end of the thirteenth century, Mycenaean culture in Greece and the dynasties in the Near East and Egypt were all threatened by new attackers. These seafaring marauders from the north – the *polis* Greeks thought them Dorians; modern archaeologists prefer 'sea peoples' – fought primarily on foot and in mass formation, without expensive chariotry, horses, or highly trained javelin-throwers and bowmen. And these northerners – as in case of the Spanish

Almost all ceramic representation of Greek mythology dates from the period of the polis, *when the Olympians were often portrayed on pots as battling against a variety of less civilized adversaries, ranging from giants – as seen here on an Attic red-figure krater of about 460 – to Amazons, centaurs, and monsters. Combatants were often represented in varying degrees of hoplite dress, emphasizing the symbolic dominance of the male landowning citizen in the city state.*

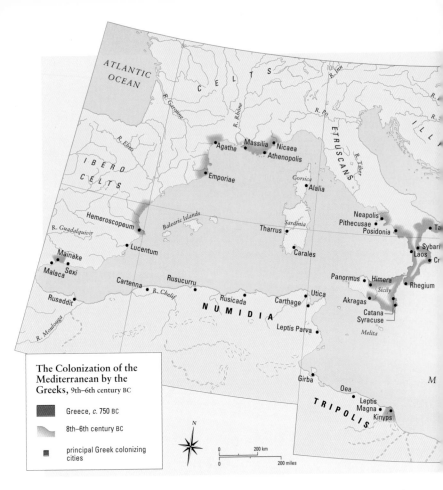

The Colonization of the Mediterranean by the Greeks, 9th–6th century BC

Greece, c. 750 BC

8th–6th century BC

principal Greek colonizing cities

0   200 km

0   200 miles

conquistadors nearly three millennia later in the Americas – learned that their flexible infantry tactics could overturn the entire military arm of a highly centralized regime.

In response to such aggression, we see for the first time the dramatic appearance of newer Mycenaean armour designed to be worn on foot, not on a chariot, and the simultaneous appearance, by at least 1200, of greaves, helmets, and round shields worked variously in bronze, wood and leather. Javelins, spears and large cut-and-thrust swords also become more plentiful. Vases suggest that the very last generations of Mycenaeans were reacting to foreign military challenges – if belatedly

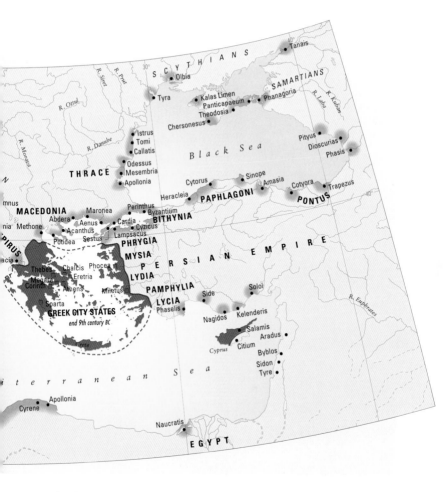

Greek culture spread throughout the Mediterranean due to Hellenic economic and political dynamism, but also because of Greek excellence in arms. From the earliest times, hoplites were prized mercenaries throughout Asia and Egypt, and Greek warships ranged freely from the southern coast of Western Europe to the Phoenician seaboard.

at least in a most radical way – by retooling and rethinking their entire military doctrine more along the lines of massed infantry. Throughout the thirteenth century the palace overlords – who designed, owned and stockpiled Mycenaean weaponry – must have learned that the prior tactics of chariot-based fighting and skirmishing were no match for well-armed, numerous and cohesive foot soldiers.

Despite this last-ditch change in weapons and tactics, by 1100 almost all citadels on the Greek mainland were destroyed and Mycenaean culture finally ended. This cataclysm of the early twelfth century has been ascribed to various causes: invaders, internal feuding, slave revolts, earthquakes, drought, piracy, or simple systems collapse caused by over-bureaucratization. Whatever the correct explication, there is less controversy that an assorted group of 'sea peoples' appear in Hittite texts and on Egyptian reliefs as barbarian hordes who sailed from the north, landed and challenged palatial kingdoms with mass infantry attacks. The later Greeks remembered them as Dorians, the sons of Heracles who destroyed everything in their path before settling in the Peloponnese. In any case, the sheer rigidity and over-complexity of the Mycenaeans left their palaces ill-prepared and inflexible against evolving tactics and armament of Hellenic-speaking but uncivilized fighters from northern hamlets outside the control of the citadels.

The military lessons were clear enough: loosely organized men, on foot, with heavy armour, were a match for chariotry, bowmen and centralized bureaucracy, Cyclopean walls or not. The Mycenaeans' eleventh-hour turn toward armoured infantry with spears was apparently too late to save the palaces, and they went the way of similar planned societies in the southern and eastern Mediterranean which also were weakened or toppled by 'barbarian' infantry. And while archaeologists often talk of a 'catastrophe' that brought on the destruction of an entire culture, from a strictly military standpoint the sudden end to a collective autocracy changed for ever the direction of Greek warfare. For the first time, the very space, time, equipment and purpose of warfare passed from the autocrat in the citadel into the hands of the individual, in a manner previously unseen in the Mediterranean.

Thus the birth of western warfare first begins with the destruction of the entire Mycenaean culture on the Greek mainland. Never again would a collective theocracy field a uniformly Greek-speaking army – in marked contrast to almost every other culture in the Mediterranean. The stage was set for a four-centuries-long political and economic evolution that would culminate in the appearance of a free citizen, who alone determined where and how men like himself would fight.

PLUNDERING AND RAIDING IN THE GREEK DARK AGES

Yet between the Mycenaean citadel and Greek city state falls a shadow. For the next 400 years (1200–800) Greece lapsed into a Dark Age. Writing vanished, monumental architecture disappeared, and population declined to perhaps less than a fifth of its previous Mycenaean high. Centralized government was lost, and with it most long-distance trade and well-organized agricultural regimens. Pictorial representation largely vanished from vases. Agricultural production plummeted. In place of a palace bureaucracy, local strongmen and barons carved out spheres of influence in small fortified hamlets. Small populations were no longer fixed and often migrated when threatened. The effects on Greek culture were far more catastrophic than the collapse of Roman civilization seventeen centuries later.

Our only sure evidence for four centuries of fighting rests mostly with a few partial remains of arms and armour uncovered from aristocratic burials. At Lefkandi on the island of Euboea and at Salamis in Cyprus such tombs reveal aristocratic fighters, interred along with their iron weapons and horses. Dark Age warfare – as Aristotle implied of all pre-*polis* fighting – apparently revolved around such mounted strong men, who led into battle loosely organized infantrymen, armed with leather and wicker shields and spears, javelins and arrows. While greaves and most metallic body armour seem to have disappeared in the wreckage of Mycenaean civilization, there was a surprising increase in iron-working in the Dark Ages, lending a new destructiveness to the old Mycenaean long sword and spear. The fifth-century historian Thucydides recalled this murky time before the *polis*, 'There were no wars by land, not at least by which power was acquired.' And he emphasized that there were no large confederations, no stable populations of tree and vine farmers, no extended campaigns, no real fighting other than local squabbling between rival neighbours. In such pre-state societies, vengeance, blood-feuds, raids in search of livestock and women, and punitive strikes, rather than carefully orchestrated expeditions to conquer and annexe territory, characterized most 'war'.

Yet the impoverishment and loss of civilization in the Dark Ages represents a distinct liberation of sorts for both agriculture and warfare. Raiders from the north may have destroyed Mycenaean palaces and civilization, but they also did away with rigid and centralized religious and political bureaucracy. Metal body armour and greaves may have been lost by their impoverished successors, but iron-working and the rising importance of foot soldiers offered the chance for superior infantry, should material culture recover and population increase. It is no accident that the destruction of rigid Mycenaean protocols of the palace gave way to a new emphasis on foot soldiers, iron weaponry, and an end to chariotry, marking a sharp break from the centralized battle practice elsewhere in the Mediterranean which lasted for the next two millennia.

The stage was now set for the slow, centuries-long evolution toward the *polis*. The loose bands of leather-protected serfs of the Dark Ages, who followed their mounted lords into battle, would finally metamorphose into real militias of small property-owning farmers with no other allegiance but to themselves. Grievances and insults to the clan that arose over theft of livestock or grazing rights would give way to civic mobilization in response to foreign intrusion on to private property.

The first and last recorded battle of the Greek Dark Ages occurred on the island of Euboea, between the rival cities of Chalkis and Eretria over the adjacent rich Lelantine plain some time before 700. We have no real idea how long the fighting lasted or who was the immediate winner. But later poets and historians considered the Lelantine fighting the first historical Greek war, an encounter known from trustworthy sources free of myth-making. Coming at the end of the Dark Ages, the Lelantine battle must have marked the final transition from an aristocratic horse war to broader-based infantry combat. And although our sources sometimes present contradictory views, it is clear that both Euboean cities had inaugurated radical changes in their military and political structure.

Ostensibly the Lelantine clash was a quarrel over turf between the aristocratic *hippeis* (cavalrymen) of Eretria and their like counterparts at Chalkis, the *hippobatae* (horse-raisers). Yet the contemporary poet Archilochus says that the Euboeans were famed for sword-play, not cavalry charges. Pottery of the era from Eretria depicts helmeted warriors, with round shields and spears, and confirms the picture of early armoured infantry prowess. The later geographer Strabo claimed he saw a centuries-old treaty recording the two sides' agreement not to use long-range weapons at all.

Consequently, a large part of both armies must have been heavy-armed infantry (*hoplitai*), who relied on spears, and, at close quarters, on swords as well. Some fighters, as contemporary vases suggest, may have been aristocratic lords who rode into battle and then dismounted to join their inferiors in the mass. Many infantrymen may not have been spearmen, but rather used multiple javelins and threw them at a distance. But in any case, infantry battle over the possession of a countryside rich in trees and vines would be the hallmark of Greek warfare for the next four centuries. And the Lelantine war proved to be the hallmark of all later Greek warfare in a more ominous sense as well. A number of Greek states intervened – most notably, Miletus on the side of Eretria, the island of Samos for Chalcis – proving that an ostensible border skirmish between two city states might ignite a full-scale war involving much of the Greek-speaking world. Gone were the days when either the palace or aristocratic horse-lord and his small circle might govern the time and space of Greek battle.

THE HOMERIC BATTLEFIELD

Homer's monumental epic the *Iliad*, composed orally some time in the late eighth century, is the first work of literature in western civilization. Because nearly a third of the poem's more than 15,600 lines is devoted to graphic descriptions of battle, and because the *Iliad* is ostensibly the tale of an even earlier raid by Greek heroes against Troy, military historians pore over the text to reconstruct fighting in the age before the city state. Unfortunately, the Homeric battlefield is confused and contradictory, and apparently an amalgam of military customs and practices fashioned from some five centuries of bardic improvisation.

Bronze-clad warriors of status are chauffeured into battle on fine chariots by personal henchmen. They dismount and are left by their drivers to fight solo on foot. Usually such Greek and Trojan grandees as Diomedes or Hector – the so-called *basileis* – criss-cross the battlefield, hunting for blue-blooded opponents whose killing or capture for ransom might add to their own prestige. Once found, the enemy warrior is usually formally – and quite rhetorically – addressed, insulted, and then targeted by the thrown spear. If the cast misses or fails to penetrate the victim's shield or body armour, the Homeric hero nearly always draws his sword and rushes forward to finish the struggle at close quarters – either way, heads roll, eyes are put out, guts spilled, and limbs whacked off. Yet such graphic battle descriptions are remarkably brief. Of some 300 in the *Iliad*, only eighteen involve more than a single blow, suggesting the hit-and-run nature of the fighting. Archers are specialized fighters both feared as lethal adversaries who can kill good men from afar, and yet despised as cowards who avoid the face-to-face fighting – a generally held opinion often with unfortunate ramifications for vulnerable western armies for the next millennium.

Massed chariot attacks, determined siegecraft, and cavalry charges are dimly known to Homeric fighters, but they are not emphasized by the poet. His chief interest is the private duelling of the front-line fighters, the *promachoi* who range out beyond the multitude (*plêthus*). When warriors are not engaged on the plain of Troy, they drink, pout, squabble, and brag or revile each other with exaggerated tales of loot that they have stolen on punitive plundering raids. What tactics, what technology, and what historical period does Homer's peculiar and often absurd brand of fighting represent?

The *Iliad* was probably composed about 700, and Homer's other extant epic the *Odyssey* followed about a quarter of a century later.

The extant walls of Troy offer a disappointing contrast with Homer's grandiose description in the Iliad, where Hector greets his wife and son far above the fray. Nevertheless, the eastern entryway pictured here, built in the fourteenth and thirteenth centuries, was probably as impressive as its Cyclopean counterparts on the Greek mainland.

Both poems were products of a long oral tradition that ultimately derived from the end of the Mycenaean era (1200–1100). Consequently, the half-millennium genesis of the epics leaves military historians in a quandary. Does the martial world of Achilles, Agamemnon and Ajax preserve the essential story of an organized Mycenaean expedition to Troy, a massive quest for metals, fishing rights, horses or land by the palace lords of the mainland? The later misfortunes of the victorious Greek kings – Agamemnon, Menelaus, Odysseus, Ajax and Diomedes either do not reach home or find their return horrific and the conditions at their palaces radically changed – perhaps reflect the tumult of the last generation of Mycenaeans, who about half a century after the sack of Troy did lose their own citadels to encroachers.

Or does the *Iliad's* fighting on the plain of Troy exaggerate some Dark Age plundering raid, in which marauding and squabbling pirates joined together for one big haul? Or is the expedition to retrieve Helen merely an outline of inherited fiction that the poetic genius Homer fleshes out with plot, action, detail, and material culture drawn from his own late eight-century world of the *polis*? Or, finally, is the poem simply a fantasy of talking horses, battling gods and personified rivers, in which 500 years of yarn are spliced together randomly to meet the poetic and metrical exigencies of epic formula?

While the *Iliad* and *Odyssey* do show traces of two earlier cultures – some authentic Mycenaean material together with many more elements of the Dark Ages – the poems are probably a rough portrait of Greece between 750 and 680, and thus give our first glimpse of war at the very end of the Dark Ages. There are only a few Mycenaean artifacts that derive from the world before the cataclysm of 1200 – a boar's-tooth helmet, long silver-studded swords, the presence of chariotry, bronze-edged weapons, large leather tower shields, massive citadel walls, the notion of a horse-rearing people on the coast of Asia Minor, and warrior names such as Ajax. These Mycenaean relics were either passed on from generation to generation through an oral tradition after the cataclysm, or were known by later bards from subsequent chance discoveries of tombs, vases and ruined palaces. What may have been a perfunctory raid against Asia Minor in the last generation of the palaces grew to a legendary feat of arms. In the impoverished conditions that followed the Mycenaean collapse, bards sang of an earlier age when Mycenaeans did things that a contemporary Dark Age audience could only dream of.

Granted, some details in the poems surely derive from the Dark Ages (1100–800). The knowledge of iron, the cremation of bodies, throwing spears, tripods, the frequent quarrels over gifts and plunder by petty chiefs were added to the epic tradition by Homer's predecessors during the centuries of Dark Age transmission. Nestor, for example, describes a raid against Elis that must have been typical pre-state battle practice, reflecting both the interest in acquisition and the honour that accrued from stealth and military prowess:

> We drove off much booty, fifty herds each of oxen, swine and goats. We took as many flocks of sheep. We also took one hundred and fifty bay horses, all female, along with many of their colts. We drove them at night right into Pylos, Neleus's

land, into the fortress during the night. Neleus was pleased
that I had gotten so much spoil though a youth.

Nevertheless, the core of Homeric society is largely a world of
assemblies, councils, colonization, mass fighting and intensive
agriculture, in which comrades struggle for their own fatherland – a
poetic cosmos that is still recognizable as the early *polis*: the poet has
inherited a very old story with plot, characters, and a few archaic
details, but the material and literary contents of the poem are mostly
from his own time and space.

So for all the poetic licence of individual duelling and boasting in the
Iliad, for all the necessary anachronism and aristocratic formality, the
careful reader can see in the shadows the charge of massed armoured
infantrymen not unlike those of early hoplite warfare. Men are often
described in files and rows (*phalanges*, *stiches*). They are outfitted in
heavy bronze armour somewhat like that worn by the citizenry of
Homer's own culture of the *polis*. In Book Sixteen of the *Iliad* we read:

> And as a man builds solid a wall with stones set close together
> for the rampart of a high house keeping out the force of the
> winds, so close together were the helms and shields massive in
> the middle. For shield leaned on shield, helmet on helmet, man
> against man, and the horse-hair crests along the horns of the
> shining helmets touched as they bent their heads, so dense
> were they formed on each other.

Even the peculiar role of chariotry, missiles and javelins in Homer does
not suggest authentic Mycenaean or Dark Age warfare. It is more
likely that these haphazard weapons and tactics again reflect Homer's
poetic need for deliberate archaizing, his often fuzzy efforts to insert
things he has heard or seen relating to the distant past. Hence warriors
heave huge boulders and taxi out in impressive chariots, all of which
lend a sense of epic majesty to the otherwise anonymous mass killing

before Troy. Battle descriptions, as in all epic poetry, must naturally center on a few notables, requiring the poet to focus unrealistically on isolated and unconnected episodes of the killing before Troy. It is difficult, after all, to compose an epic poem about an instantaneous mass collision of anonymous soldiers.

Consequently Homer's Trojan war presents fighting as a collision of two massed armies in bronze armour, not so very different from the

In vase-paintings, hoplite equipment appears pristine and comfortable.
In fact, greaves were constructed of thin pliable bronze and may have been
snapped on around the calves without laces. Helmets were so heavy and
hot that they were not put on until seconds before actual battle. Spears
were unwieldy; their length and sharp points and butt-spikes made them
dangerous during peacetime. Shields were radically concave and their
3-foot diameters and 20-pound weights made them hard to handle.

great phalanx crashes of the early seventh century – sheer havoc that is always portrayed graphically as destructive and hateful. But as an epic poet, Homer also must emphasize the mystique of the past and he must focus on individual heroism. And those constraints explain in large part the mish-mash of spear-casting, formal insults, chariot taxis, and huge leather shields – the necessary poetic veneer that decorates the more mundane massed infantry fighting of anonymous men in bronze.

Homer, then, tells us everything and nothing about early Greek warfare. A Mycenaean raid becomes exaggerated in the subsequent centuries of widespread impoverishment, depopulation and illiteracy. Itinerant stewards of the saga earned their keep by entertaining and flattering aristocratic audiences of the Dark Ages with epic songs about their reputed ancestors' duelling and feuding – entertainment not unlike the current Rap hits that glorify rival gangs who shoot and maim each other for prestige, women, booty and turf. Yet all such earlier oral poets of the Dark Ages are lost to the historical record, and it is only Homer – composing in the first generation of the *polis* at a time of growing literacy – who fashions the old stories into a monumental epic that appeals to his peers because it raises issues and dilemmas that only men of the nascent city state could grasp.

The *Iliad*, remember, is a great story of the immature Achilles and his slow evolution toward self-realization and enlightenment – the best men in war are not always appreciated, the material rewards of mass killing are sometimes hollow, and both enemy and friend share a common humanity that transcends their feuds over less important issues of the passing day. True, the poem presents us with a frightening example of early western warfare – armoured men in rank, appalling carnage, shock tactics, group discipline, and open debate over strategy and tactics. But the dilemma of Achilles also inaugurates a peculiarly Greek approach to warfare that could arise only in a consensual society where speech is free and expression unchecked: the destructiveness of Greek arms from now on will raise questions among these same free-thinking Greeks about the very wisdom and morality of war itself.

CHAPTER TWO

The Rise of the City State and the Invention of Western Warfare (750–490)

Argument still rages whether the Athenian Parthenon and the other buildings on the acropolis were built from local revenues or were the dividends of the forced contributions of the subject states of the Athenian empire. Yet, unlike monumental building elsewhere in the Mediterranean, during the Classical period such expensive temples were never used exclusively for religious purposes, much less as tombs for theocratic or royal rulers. Rather, these religious shrines doubled as utilitarian state archives, civic treasuries, and armouries for state-owned military equipment. The Parthenon is seen here from the Temple of Nike; to the left is a corner of the majestic roofed gateway to the acropolis, the Propylae.

The coming of the Hoplite

By 700 GREEK RECOVERY from more than four centuries of cultural obscurity was well under way. Nearly 1,000 small, autonomous communities now dotted the Greek-speaking world from southern Italy to the Black Sea. Population growth may have reached 2 to 3 per cent per annum in some years. Colonies and trading posts were founded throughout the Mediterranean. Maritime commerce with Phoenicia and Egypt was renewed on an increased scale. Writing re-emerged, but was now based on an improved Phoenician alphabet, far more useful and accessible to the population at large than the arcane record-keeping Linear B script of the Mycenaean palaces. Written constitutions appeared in the great majority of city states and their colonies, ensuring the spread of government by consensus of landed peers. The Greek countryside itself was no longer a pasture for sheep, goats and horses, but now more often a patchwork of small 10-acre farms of trees, vines and grain, often with an isolated homestead to house its ever vigilant and independent owner, a citizen who alone in the Mediterranean had clear legal rights to land tenure, property inheritance – and his own arms.

Just as Greek city states and their surrounding satellite villages grew to service the burgeoning agricultural community and to facilitate expanding trade, so too the hills outside the *polis* were gradually reclaimed and terraced. Growing numbers of ubiquitous farmers sought empty land wherever they could, whether on the mountains near the city state or through external colonization in pristine territory overseas. As land and property were dispersed to a new class beyond the control of

A Persian at Thermopylae would have faced a Spartan hoplite that looked exactly as represented by this bronze statuette from the late sixth or early fifth century. The hoplite's greaves, leather flaps beneath his midriff, bronze breastplate, helmet and enormous crest give him a good chance at surviving the mêlée. Notice the long hair that flows from his helmet – a Spartan trademark that so astonished the Persians, who saw King Leonidas and his men calmly combing their locks before their last and fatal charge into the pass.

aristocratic horsemen, as landed councils replaced aristocratic cabals, as livestock raising was overshadowed by intensive agriculture, as metalworking turned from the tripods of the wealthy to the arms and farming implements of middling agrarians, so too was the practice of Greek warfare made anew.

The evidence of this seventh- and sixth-century military renaissance – literary, pictorial and archaeological – is piecemeal, but when taken as a whole it represents a revolutionary shift in the nature of conflict and society, the first emergence in European culture, or in any other culture, of a large group of middling landowners who craft a military agenda to reflect their own agrarian needs. There were now novel words in the Greek vocabulary – *politês*, *politeia*, *hoplitês*, *mesos* – for 'citizen', 'constitution', 'hoplite militiaman' and 'middling man' to reflect radically new concepts, as an entire agrarian class (*zeugitai*) now monopolized infantry service. Early Corinthian vase-painters, such as the anonymous artist of the so-called Chigi vase (*c.* 650), show armoured spearmen advancing in lock-step to the music of flutes. At the Panhellenic sanctuaries in Olympia and Delphi votive offerings of bronze helmets, breastplates and greaves

Early sixth-century Greek hoplite headgear was heavy, bucket-like and ill-fitting, but still provided wonderful protection for the head, face and neck. Cast in one piece of bronze, this so-called Corinthian helmet had interior leather protection stitched to the inside. A large horsehair crest was fitted to a bronze holder at the apex of the helmet. The nose-guards are frequently found bent or missing, since captured helmets were often dedicated to the gods with clear indications that they were taken from the vanquished.

proliferate – over 100,000 bronze helmets may conceivably have been dedicated between 700 and 500. The lyric poets Tyrtaeus, Callinus and Alcaeus elaborate on the haphazard Homeric references to heavy infantrymen, with an accompanying creed that men are to fight side-by-side, 'toe-to-toe, shield-against-shield' against the enemy, winning in their 'gleaming bronze and nodding crests' glory for their families and state, rather than for themselves alone. Inscriptions on stone, stray graffiti, and an oral tradition even record the presence of such prized Greek and Carian mercenary infantry – 'the men in bronze' – as far away as Persia and Egypt.

Consequently, in the seventh and sixth centuries most decisive fighting that put an end to disputes between developing Greek city states was by heavy infantry composed of farmers outfitted in bronze armour with thrusting spears. Intensively worked vineyards, orchards and grainfields were now privately held, increasingly valued, and served an ever-growing population. If a community was self-supporting through, and governed by, its surrounding private landowners, then hoplite warfare, far better than fortification or garrisoning passes, made perfect sense: muster the largest, best-armed group (*pandêmei*) of farmers to protect land in the quickest, cheapest and most decisive way possible. It was far easier and more economical for farmers to defend farmland on farmland than to tax and hire landless others endlessly to guard passes – the sheer ubiquity of which in mountainous Greece ensured that they could usually be crossed by enterprising invaders anyway. Raiding, ambush and plundering, of course, were still common – such activities seem innate to the human species – but the choice of military response to win or protect territory was now a civic matter, an issue to be voted on by free landowning infantrymen themselves.

As such, hoplite fighting through shock collision marks the true beginning of western warfare, a formal idea now fraught with legal, ethical and political implications. Almost all these wars of a day between rugged and impatient yeomen were infantry encounters over land, usually disputed border strips involving agrarian prestige more than prized fertility. Customarily the army of one city state, an Argos, Thebes or Sparta, met their adversary in daylight in formal columnar formation – the word phalanx means 'rows' or 'stacks' of men – according to a recognized sequence of events.

After divination, a seer sacrificed a ram to the god. The 'general' (*stratêgos*) made a brief exhortation, and then the assembled infantry prepared to charge the enemy. In minutes the respective armies packed together to achieve a greater density of armed men (*hoplitai, stratiôtai*), who sought to crash together, sometimes trotting the last 200 yards between the two phalanxes. For the defenders it was often on the same soil they and their neighbours had worked a few days

Greek armies habitually sacrificed animals – sheep and goats mostly – to various gods before crossing rivers, approaching the enemy, or charging across the battlefield. Whether the slaughtered animal was a thank-offering or killed for divination purposes mattered little: the seer's activity usually sanctified the actual conditions of the battlefield. Thus few victorious armies felt a need to apologize to the gods, even fewer passed up a sure victory because the prebattle signs were 'unfavourable'.

before. For the invaders, the farmhouses, orchards, vineyards and stone field walls were largely identical to their own plots back home. Once a neighbouring community had fashioned a force of armoured columns (*phalanges*) to take or hold flatland, there was very little a like-minded rival could do other than to meet the challenge in about the same manner.

After the meeting of phalanxes, farmers, blinded by the dust and their own cumbersome helmets, stabbed away with their spears, screamed the war-cry (*eleleu!* or *alala!*), pushed on ahead with their shields, and, failing that, grabbed, kicked and bit, desperately hoping to make some inroad into the enemy's phalanx, usually having little idea who, if any, they had killed or wounded. Success was at first gauged by the degree of motion achieved by the pushing of the ranks – the literal thrusting of a man's shield upon the shoulders, side or back of his comrade ahead. There were few feints, reserves, encircling maneuovres, or sophisticated tactics of any kind in hoplite battle before the latter fifth century – just the frightful knowledge that a man must plough through the spears across the plain.

Only the first three ranks of the eight rows of the classical phalanx reached the enemy with their spears in the first assault. When they broke, they went hand-to-hand with swords and their butt-spikes. Later tactical writers stress just how important such front-line fighters were in achieving an initial inroad. Once the phalanx ripped and stormed through the ranks of its adversary, the opponent often totally collapsed through panic and fright, perhaps not more than half an hour after the initial collision. The short duration and sudden disintegration of battle are understandable if we keep in mind that combatants were squeezed together in columns, trapped in heavy bronze under the summer sun, mostly robbed of sight and hearing, in a sea of dust and blood – the captives, as the historian Thucydides reminds us, of rumour and their own fears.

Still, there were countless tasks for all infantrymen of the phalanx as it pounded the enemy. Hoplites – the name probably derives from *hopla*, the Greek word for their heavy battle gear – in the initial ranks sought targets with their spears, all the while searching for protection for their vulnerable right flanks in the round shields of the men at their sides. Some struggled to step over the debris of fallen equipment and the detritus of the wounded and dead at their feet, striving always to keep their balance as they pushed and were pushed into the enemy spears at their faces.

All the hoplites in the killing zone kept their own 20-pound shield chest high to cover themselves and the men on their own immediate left. Thus all at once hoplites might feel steady pressure from the rear, dodge enemy spearpoints and friendly spear-butts jostling in their faces, stab and push ahead, accommodate comrades shoving from the left to find protection, seek their own cover by nudging to friends' shields on their right, and nearly trip over wounded bodies, corpses, and abandoned equipment that was lying at their feet.

The ranks of the phalanx could not be broken by either advancing light infantry or horsemen – as long as the ground was level and discipline was maintained. In theory, the phalanx kept neat order; in reality, rows and files intermingled with one another, as pressure from the enemy sent soldiers crashing into each other and phalangites scrambled to fill gaps caused by the fallen.

Once the line cracked hoplites turned, scattered, and ran to prevent encirclement and probable annihilation, but few of the victorious pressed the chase to any great distance. Heavy infantrymen make poor pursuers, especially when the defeated threw away their equipment and sprinted to the hills. And under the war practice of early city state warfare, there was not much desire anyway to exterminate an adversary who spoke the same language, worshipped identical gods, observed common festivals, and enjoyed similar types of government by landowning citizens. Again, the primary purpose was to acquire or take back border real estate and gain prestige, not to risk time and money in annihilating a neighbouring society of like-armoured farmers over the hill.

After hoplite battle, the dead were not desecrated but exchanged, in what Euripides called 'the custom of all the Greeks'. Greek painting and sculpture – in contrast, for example, to Near Eastern, Egyptian or MesoAmerican engravings – reveal almost no mutilation of corpses in a wartime context. A formal trophy was erected, and the victors marched home to congratulations. The defeated begged for the remains of their comrades to be returned formally to be buried in a common grave on the battlefield or carried back home to a public tomb. If the battle was exclusively between Greek hoplites and before the fifth century, then rarely were the vanquished enslaved – quite unlike the great sieges and later wars of annihilation against non-Greeks, in which thousands were sold off as chattels in consequence of defeat.

Still, the battlefield was a gory place. Xenophon, for example, records the carnage after second Coronea (394):

> The earth was stained with blood, and the remains of friends and enemies lay side-by-side. There were shattered shields, broken spears, and unsheathed swords, some lying about on the ground, others stuck in corpses, and others still gripped as if to strike even in death.

The Spartans must have had some idea of the butchery of hoplite fighting when they wore wooden 'dog-tags' around their necks to ensure the later identification of mangled corpses. No wonder we hear of soldiers drinking wine before battle, a characteristic of pre-battle from Homer to Alexander the Great's march into Asia.

Such fighting between city states could be frequent but not necessarily catastrophic, once cavalry and missile-men were largely excluded from any integrated role in the fighting and the infantry combatants were uniformly encased in bronze. And while it is true that Plato and other Greek thinkers felt that war was a natural state of affairs in Greece, rather than an aberration from accustomed tranquillity, their notion of war, *polemos*, was much different from our own. Only the Persian and Peloponnesian conflicts of the Classical Age, which inaugurate a second stage in the development of western warfare, conjure up anything like the modern idea that fighting is intended entirely to destroy armies, murder civilians, kill thousands of soldiers and wreck culture – and so to be an uninterrupted, all-encompassing activity until ultimate victory through annihilation or capitulation was achieved. In the first two centuries of hoplite fighting (700–490), it was enough, as the philosophers noted, every so often to kill a small portion of the enemy in an afternoon crash, crack his morale, and send him scurrying in defeat and shame from whence he came.

The Greeks, then, for a brief time practised a quasi-ritualized warfare in which fighting was frequent but did not seem to imperil the cultural, economic and political renaissance of the Hellenic city state – even at the height of the hoplite age it was rare for more than 10 per cent of the men who fought that day to die. If anything, the sheer terror of hoplite battle, the courage needed to stare at a wall of spears across the plain, and the urgency for group solidarity in the confines of the phalanx gave positive momentum to ideas of civic responsibility and egalitarianism, and formed the emotional and spiritual substructure of much of archaic Greek sculpture, painting and literature. Nearly every major Greek author, philosopher or statesman, despite their education and often élite status, served with their fellow citizens in the front lines of battle: Archilochus, Tyrtaeus, Aeschylus, Miltiades, Themistocles, Aristides, Sophocles, Pericles, Socrates, Thucydides, Alcibiades, Xenophon, Demosthenes, and others too frequent to mention at some time wore a breastplate and killed another human – something historians and literary critics should always keep in mind when they assess the character and ideology of Greek politics, art, philosophy and literature.

Because originally the battle line was composed exclusively of the landowning citizenry of various allied small city states – hamlets mustered their phalanxes side-by-side in a long row – the course of a particular engagement and the ensuing hoplite casualties could often have enormous political and demographic ramifications. While general losses might be moderate, nevertheless particular contingents could be wiped out if they bore the brunt of a concentrated enemy thrust or were stationed opposite superior troops. At Marathon, and then again at Plataea, the Athenian tribe Aiantis seems to have been hit hard by the Persian assault, and probably bore a disproportionate percentage of the dead, with lasting consequences for a small number of families generations hence. The tiny community of Thespiae had most of its male population wiped out at Thermopylae (480) and again at Delium (424); in the aftermath of both those losses its city walls were demolished by invaders. In the case of the latter battle, the stationing of the Thespians directly in the path of the crack troops of the enemy, and the destruction of their city the next year by their own 'allies', the Thebans, were probably not unrelated phenomena. Aristotle pointed out that radical democracy was strengthened in the mid fifth century when Athenian hoplites were away suffering inordinate casualties on expedition – allowing the landless at home to force through more democratic reforms. The loss of 400 élite Spartiates with their king at Leuctra (371), who were obliterated by

Epaminondas' deep phalanx, weakened for ever the entire structure of Spartan apartheid. And at the first battle of Mantinea (418), the Spartans may have deliberately preferred to punish the more liberal of their Argive adversaries on the theory that their destruction would help to facilitate a return to oligarchy – and hence a renewed Argive alliance with Sparta. Under the brutal circumstances of shock battle, a single day's carnage often changed the very political fabric of communities for subsequent decades.

Controversy still rages over the origins of such peculiar hoplite infantrymen, who were as suspicious of mounted aristocrats as they were of impoverished skirmishers, who in a mountainous country fought exclusively on small plains, and who wore heavy bronze armour in the Greek summer and early autumn. Did their panoply emerge piecemeal between 725 and 700, followed decades later by the tactics of the phalanx itself (*c.* 650)? Or were the hoplites' new weapons a technological response to *existing* mass fighting? And is the city state itself to be explained by the rise of revolutionary hoplite infantrymen, who forced aristocratic concessions through the solidarity of their columns? Or, finally, were early hoplites a conservative and aristocratic force, who gradually evolved from mounted grandees and had little to do with the emergence of a constitutional *polis*?

Most probably it was the technology of the panoply and not the tactics of the phalanx that were new: novel weapons improved an old way of fighting. Dark Age soldiers had for many years fought loosely in mass formation in ancient Greece, in most cases under the direction of aristocratic leaders and clansmen. Gradually the spread of diversified, intensified farming in the eighth century created a shared ideology among new landowners, men in the ranks who had begun to accumulate some capital for weapons from their farming success. With the same ingenuity by which they devised new approaches to traditional land use, the planters of trees and vines began to fabricate innovative bronze weaponry to improve their performance in the traditional mêlée of Dark Age battle. Shock troops with bronze armour and long pikes are hard to move off their land, harder still when they have enhanced their weapons for such fighting and turned their disorderly mass into ordered files and rows. Aristotle, in his *Politics*, envisions just such a sequence:

Two ingredients were critical for hoplite success: steely nerve and muscular strength. In this mid fifth-century red-figure vase-painting, the focused gaze and strong right arm of the bearded warrior are understandably emphasized. The 20-pound weight of the concave shield could not be maintained by the arm alone, so it was often rested on the left shoulder as seen here. Long hair and beards were liabilities when the fighting progressed to hand-to-hand, but the hair may have cushioned the weight of the helmet and, along with the crest and ornamentation of the headgear, lent a ferocity to the appearance of the hoplite. In such a formalized method of fighting, in which opposing armies stared at each other before the collision, the image of savagery was critical.

> The earliest form of government among the Greeks after monarchy was composed of those who actually fought. In the beginning that meant cavalry, since without cohesive arrangement, heavy armament is useless; and experience and tactical knowledge of these systems did not exist in ancient times, and so power again lay with mounted horsemen. But once the *poleis* grew and those with hoplite armour became stronger, more people shared in government.

Aristotle suggests that hoplite fighting is to be connected with the transition from mounted aristocracy to the rule of middling landowners, once hoplite armour refined the traditional mass into the cohesive ranks of the phalanx.

Military technology in itself rarely if ever invents tactics; more often new designs are responses to existing needs. Consequently, we should imagine that Greeks throughout the Dark Ages fought in loose bands of poorly protected skirmishers who followed mounted nobles into battle. As such serfs became detached from aristocratic houses and set off on their own, they would gain the means to craft their weapons to meet their own needs as ground fighters: better armour and stout thrusting spears. Most obviously, rectangular hide shields were replaced by circular ones of strong oak, the extra weight in part handled by a new double grip. Linen or leather corselets gave way to bronze, and javelins and two spears were superseded by a single tough cornel-wood spear with an iron tip. The concavity of the round hoplite shield, the backplate of bronze and the addition of a spike to the bottom of the spear are more subtle refinements that reflect the needs of those in the middle and rear ranks who might rest their shields on their shoulders, push on the men ahead and use their spears' butt-ends to dispatch prostrate enemies as they marched.

Hoplite technology is not, then, a dramatic revolution that creates the city state though the superior weaponry of a new military class. Rather it is a reflection of the fact that middling agrarians were already established and now dictated the entire rules and rituals of Greek warfare, crafting novel weapons and protocols to ensure the exclusivity of yeoman infantry under the traditional Greek practices of massed attack.

And there was nothing quite like hoplite equipment anywhere in the Mediterranean, suggesting that only a free citizenry would craft, wear and maintain such cumbersome weapons that might total half the wearer's weight. Chauvinism about their use is present in nearly all Greek literature. Homer, the lyric poets, Herodotus and Aeschylus all brag about the superiority and ostentation of Greek plate, nodding crests and iron-tipped spears. But while the 50–70 pounds of wood, iron and bronze gave unmatched safety, the ensemble was also a curse: uncomfortable, ponderous, hot, impeding motion and nullifying most of its wearer's senses. Aristophanes joked that the breastplate was better used as a chamber pot, the shield as a well-cover.

There were no holes for hearing in the massive Corinthian helmet, no netting or interior suspension to cushion blows to the head. Instead, the wearer had only some stitched leather inside and his

This classical hoplite helmet, found in a grave excavated at Corinth, represents the climax of the so-called Corinthian design. Its sleek cheek and neck guards, the eerie cut-outs for the eyes, and the impressed ridge at the top of the face gave unmatched protection and lent a sense of terror to the warrior. Yet by the latter third of the fifth century, many hoplites found such Corinthian helmets either too cumbersome or too expensive as war grew increasingly more mobile and engaged a larger number of combatants.

own hair as a buffer against the rough bronze. Spear-thrusts to the head bruised the brain. The helmet's narrow eye-slits cut off peripheral vision. And the massive horsehair crest, while lending a sense of ferocity to its otherwise diminutive owner and deflecting blows from above, must have further obstructed the vision of others in the phalanx, and made the bulky and top-heavy helmet even more awkward. Indeed, vase-paintings occasionally show hoplites who are implausibly grabbed and pulled by their crests. By the later fifth century a conical bronze cap without facial protection was understandably preferred.

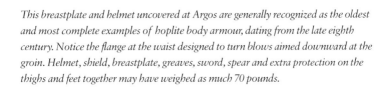

The bell corselet (*thôrax*) of a ¼-inch thickness of bronze, offered substantial protection against nearly every type of arrow, spear or sword attack, allowing Greek infantry to slice through the 'sea of spears' in a way unmatched until medieval times. Yet, most early breastplates weighed between 25 and 30 pounds. Without ventilation, they became little more than solar collectors on the summer battlefield. Stooping, sitting or rising required Herculean effort, and it is no accident that a favourite scene on both stone sculpture and ceramic painting is the scrum where soldiers stumble, fall, or lie recumbent, stuck fast in their cumbersome armour. We can only imagine how early hoplites, who originally wore additional

This breastplate and helmet uncovered at Argos are generally recognized as the oldest and most complete examples of hoplite body armour, dating from the late eighth century. Notice the flange at the waist designed to turn blows aimed downward at the groin. Helmet, shield, breastplate, greaves, sword, spear and extra protection on the thighs and feet together may have weighed as much 70 pounds.

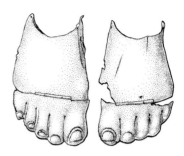

Bronze foot-guards were probably worn by officers and wealthy hoplites in the eighth and sixth centuries. But by the fifth century, such auxiliary armour – along with thigh pieces, elbow and ankle guards, and shoulder plates – were probably discarded, as warfare became more mobile and involved thousands of infantrymen.

thigh, upper-arm, ankle, stomach, and even foot armour, could even move, much less fight, under such weight – skeletal remains suggest average hoplites were not much more than 5 feet 6 inches tall, and weighed about 140 pounds. Many of the less affluent fighters must have preferred composite leather body protection, which, as armies became larger by the fifth century, became common, with reinforced leather strips dangling below to protect the groin. The ubiquitous flute players present on early vases thus seem logical – early heavily clad hoplites of the seventh and sixth centuries probably lumbered in cadence to music until the very last yards before the enemy. The reactionary Spartans always advanced to the enemy's spears at a slow walk set to flutes, and probably wore the heaviest of all panoplies well into Classical times.

The extraordinary double-gripped, concave 3-foot shield was singular; there were no circular shields of comparable size and design anywhere before or after in the Mediterranean. Greek phalanxes were calibrated by the depth of their cumulative shields – 'eight shields deep', 'twenty-five shields deep', 'fifty shields deep' – not by counting spears, nor even referring to the rows of infantrymen themselves. The shield's hand grip and arm support distributed the 16–20-pound weight along the whole arm rather than on just the hand. And the concavity of the shield – as is portrayed so commonly on Greek vases – allowed the hoplite's shoulder to be tucked under the upper shield rim: those in middle and rear ranks could rest their arms entirely as the ponderous weight fell on the body itself. Because

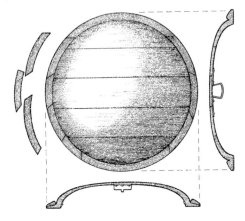

*Many scholars forget that the hoplite's shield was constructed not of bronze, but of oak planks cured and glued together to form a laminated, concave dish. A thin veneer of hammered bronze served as a faceplate to protect the wood from weathering, and to ensure that a highly polished surface might reflect the sun. The sling for the left arm (*porpax*) and the hand grip (*antilabê*) were riveted into the wood.*

of the shield's impressive circumference, its thickness was unfortunately minimal in order to reduce weight. Breakage was thus common. Throughout Greek literature we learn of the wood shield splintering or cracking. Its thin bronze face-plate – decorated by hideous blazons and later patriotic insignia – was designed mostly to inspire terror and in a practical sense to prevent weathering of the laminated wood core.

Greaves gave some protection to the shins from missile attack and downward spear thrusts. But the absence of laces may suggest that they were intended to be bent around the leg and kept in place solely by the flexibility of the bronze. A good fit was essential, and so of all the items in the panoply we should imagine that such lower leg guards were the most troublesome and so often likely to be discarded – especially when alternate long leather shield aprons were riveted to the bottom of the shield. By late Classical times only officers and the wealthy wore greaves with any frequency.

Scholars are unsure to what degree the entire panoply was worn in different periods by all members of the phalanx. Heavier armament seems to have been a hallmark of the seventh century; later, composite materials were substituted for bronze and some items cast off entirely in a slow evolutionary trend to lighten weight and gain mobility, as the size of armies grew and the nature of the enemy became less predictable. The cost to outfit a hoplite was not excessive – less than half a year's wage. The shield and spear were made of wood; and leg, arm and thigh protection was optional and rare, leaving the chief expense of the bronze helmet and breastplate well within the reach of yeoman farmers.

In addition, we are not sure whether armour was differentiated by class, rank, or position in the phalanx, although some students of military archaeology have suggested that the wealthier fighters, officers, or those in the front ranks wore complete panoplies, while the lighter clad were mostly 'pushers' to the rear, and often the poorer rank and file without status. No solid evidence supports those logical assumptions. It is at least clear from vase-painting and literature, however, that apart from Sparta most hoplites of the city state were not always uniformly armed – we should, of course, expect incongruity in militias where soldiers supplied their own arms. Infantrymen clearly did not resemble the idealized, sleek, half-nude athletes of ceramic painting. Better to imagine hoplites as grubby farmers, sometimes well into middle age – in theory eligible for some type of infantry service until sixty-two – who wore just about whatever protection that they inherited, found, swapped, or could afford, with great latitude given to personal taste, comfort, and their particular age, experience, and role in the phalanx.

The small secondary iron sword or cleaver was utilized to dispatch fallen and wounded adversaries, and provided some insurance should the spear splinter – a common scene in Greek painting and mentioned often in Classical literature. But the Greeks said 'taken by the spear', never 'by the sword', and the 7–9-foot spear was the hoplite's chief weapon, used almost exclusively for thrusting and rarely, and only in the most desperate circumstances, thrown. Because the left hand was needed for the large shield, the right alone could wield little more than the weight of an 8-foot long, 1-inch diameter wood shaft with two metal points. All ancient Greek infantry armament is governed by this often unrecognized interrelationship between the size of the shield and the length of the spear, which often reveals either the defensive or offensive ideology of a military culture – lethal heavy pikes are impossible as long as a soldier must employ his left hand to hold a large shield to protect himself and his comrades.

In contrast to the later tiny shield, fabric body armour and enormous pikes of Hellenistic phalangites, the hoplite panoply during the age of the city state put its emphasis entirely on defence – heavy breastplates, enormous shields, moderate-length spears – which reflected the agrarian conservatism of its owner. Mobility, speed, range – all the factors that promote real killing on the battlefield – were secondary to the hoplite's chief concern: group solidarity and maximum defence, crucial to cement agrarian ties and allow the farmers to push through or knock down the enemy and so get back quickly to their home plots in one piece.

In sum, the early Greek agrarian hoplite was the most cumbersome, slow – and best protected – infantryman in the entire history of western warfare. The bronze plate of the hoplite panoply stopped most spear thrusts and airborne missiles. Blows to the armoured regions of the body then most probably resulted in painful, but not necessarily fatal, contusions and bruises. Both Alexander the Great and the Macedonian Perseus, for example, suffered several wounds to the chest and head which they survived due to the presence of their bronze breastplates – throwbacks to an earlier age when all combatants, not just officers, had worn such protection.

The large shield and breastplate covered the vital organs and directed attack elsewhere. Yet even sword and spear cuts to the unprotected arms, lower legs, feet and hands, if not infected, could be treated without fatal complications. While the Greeks knew nothing of the etiology of infection, long experience had taught them that wound cleaning and bandaging could prevent complication and stem blood loss. Agesilaus, the old hoplite king of Sparta, died in his eighties of natural causes, his body a road map of old battle scars and injuries.

Vase-painting shows two favourite targets of the spear attack: the groin and thighs. Both areas, which were often left exposed beneath the moving shield, were inadequately protected by leather flaps (pteruges) riveted to the breastplate. Advancing hoplites during the initial charge and later brief pursuit more often held the spear with the underhand grip; when stationary in the ranks, or forced to stand and ward off attackers, the overhand thrust was preferred.

But battle wounds likely to kill were penetrating spear thrusts to the unprotected throat, neck, and face, thighs and groin – favourite scenes on Greek vases and a common topic in both Homeric and Greek lyric poetry. So the Dorian poet Tyrtaeus sings of the old hoplite dying while 'holding in his hands his testicles all bloody'. Especially lethal were deep puncture wounds to these areas, most likely inflicted in the first initial crash, when the running hoplite could lend momentum and real power to his inaugural spear stab. And just as serious were compound fractures inflicted in the mad pushing, when a heavily armed hoplite stumbled and was trampled and kicked by his own men – a frequent enough scene in Greek ceramic paintings and on sculpture. While Greek medicine knew sophisticated methods of setting bones and extracting projectiles, its use of lint and fabric, together with plant juices, myrrh and wine, could not staunch damage to the major arteries and internal bleeding involving the vital organs. Any hoplite who fell beneath the tumult would probably have been either kicked repeatedly or finished off with secondary thrusts from the butt-spike of the spear. Such victims most probably died in a matter of minutes from blood loss and subsequent shock.

The key to the hoplite's survival was to withstand the initial crash, stay upright, and keep the enemy at his face should there be panic and flight. If a man could just manage that, there was a good chance that his bronze would keep out deep penetration wounds, while slices, scrapes, and stabs to his arms and legs were treatable and thus often survivable.

For all the pragmatic advantages of hoplite armour, there was an undeniable element of ostentation as well, quite apart from the aesthetics of ceremonial incised armour and inlaid swords. Horsehair crests, helmets akin to terrifying masks and hideous shield blazons all lent a sense of the mysterious if not macabre to their wearer, himself usually bearded with hair dangling by his ears. When arrayed in the phalanx, the psychological effect was only magnified: bristling spears, dazzling bronze, geometric columns. Plutarch compared the phalanx to a 'ferocious beast as it wheels and stiffens its bristles'; the Spartan king Agesilaus crafted his columns to look 'like one mass of bronze and scarlet'. The hoplite was a pragmatic, hard-scrabble farmer, but he was also a warrior whose very equipment, formidable columns, and reliance on the good will of the gods lent an aura of mysticism and terror to the entire formal enterprise of phalanx battle. The English word 'panic' derived from the Greek god Pan, who was often responsible for driving hoplites to terror as they waited in the phalanx, staring across no man's land at the wall of spears which they knew they could not escape.

By the early seventh century, the seeds of later Greek and Roman military dynamism had been sown: a radically new military tradition in the West was implanted among the citizenry with its chief tenet centred around the heroic and face-to-face collision of massed armies of free citizens, in which daylight fighting, notification of intent, and the absence of ambush and manoeuvre put a high premium on nerve and muscle. At its inauguration, the practice of shock battle was embedded amid the parochialism of Greek agrarianism, whose moral protocols provided a brake on the Greek propensity to improve technology and technique. Strategy was little more than taking back borderland. Yet within a few centuries, such agrarian stricture and ritual eroded. Decisive confrontations took on the spectacle of horrendous slaughters involving soldier and civilian alike – and on terrain and for purposes never dreamed of by the original men in bronze.

THE AGRARIAN DUELS

The first detailed account of a particular hoplite engagement is not found until Herodotus' description of the battle of Marathon (490), itself written at least fifty years after the battle that involved Hellenic allied armies pitted against Persians, not two similarly armed and equipped Greek phalanxes. For the two centuries of hoplite fighting before Marathon, therefore, we must rely on vase-painting, random allusions in the lyric and elegiac poets, and second- and third-hand accounts collected by later topographers and compilers.

As we have seen, the so-called Lelantine war (*c*. 700) between the Euboean cities of Chalcis and Eretria marked the end of the Dark Ages and consisted of a fully fledged infantry conflict over borders that drew in armies from elsewhere in the Greek world. A little later in the middle of the seventh century Greek hoplite mercenaries – 'the bronze men who had come from the sea' – had established enough of a reputation to serve in Egypt under Psammetichus I (who reigned from 664–609). Indeed, we can still see the names of Greek infantrymen scratched on the left leg of the colossal statue of

Ramesses II at Abu Simbel, where they fought for pay for King Psammetichus II (*c.* 591). The seventh-century lyric poet Archilochus apparently put himself out for similar hire and laughed about the abandonment of his all-important hoplite shield. Thus by the end of the seventh century we should imagine that hoplite fighting in the phalanx was ubiquitous in Greece, its unmatched warriors becoming known as effective mercenary bands throughout the Mediterranean.

In Greece itself, given the scanty nature of our early literary sources, we naturally hear only of a few recorded early hoplite battles – and almost no fighting at sea at all. The Argive victory over Sparta at Hysiae in 669 perhaps involved the earliest heavy infantry armies on the Greek mainland, suggesting that true hoplites who fought in phalanxes first appeared in the Peloponnese – the helmet even in later times was still called 'Corinthian' and the round concave shield 'Argive'. Sparta's first (733–715?) and second (660?) wars with Messenia were infantry encounters to annexe neighbouring farmland. In all these instances, the disputes between city states arose over boundary ground and were fought by heavy infantry in column, reflecting the early symbiosis between hoplites and agriculture – and the rise of landed consensual governments.

Sometimes these early hoplite battles resembled near-ritual duels. The Persian Mardonius is made to say by Herodotus that the Greeks had an absurd, ritualistic and terrifying practice of colliding on 'the fairest and most level ground'. Therefore at the battle of Plataea (479) he vainly proposed to settle the entire Persian wars according to this Greek idea of a set duel between picked contingents. Earlier at the so-called 'Battle of Champions' (550?) where Sparta finally reversed Argive supremacy, 300 select Spartans paired up against a like number of Argive champions, the disputed land going to the corps with the last surviving warrior. And at about the same time (560–550?) we hear of a similarly formalistic 'Battle of the Fetters', when the Spartans brought along irons to bind their adversaries, but instead found themselves defeated and locked in their own chains. Even as late as 420 the Argives proposed that they should settle disagreements over their centuries-old border dispute by a formal pitched battle, in which pursuit was outlawed.

Despite the contrived nature of the battles of 'Champions' and 'Fetters' – notice the near-total annihilation in the first example, and an entire enslavement in the second – hoplite battle could still be horrific even in its ritualistic efforts to exclude civilians and non-combatants. And military rite could always be abandoned in favour of political expediency. For example, after the battle of Sepeia (494), the Spartan king Cleomenes allowed his helot baggage carriers – freeing his hoplites from incurring the pollution of slaughtering the innocent – to incinerate over 6,000 fugitive Argive infantrymen trapped in a sacred grove.

Throughout the seventh and sixth centuries most agrarian communities were making the final but difficult transition from hereditary aristocracy to broader-based oligarchies of yeoman farmers. Just as we hear of early assemblies of property-owners and egalitarian land distribution schemes, so too we imagine that hoplite warfare emphasized the same uniform nature of the new citizen: as a voter he claimed an equal seat in the assembly hall, as farmer a piece of land of about the same size as his peers, and as infantryman a slot in his regiment identical to all others. The resulting mosaic ensured stable government, a patchwork of roughly similar ancestral farm plots, and good battle order.

The set battle piece with its myriad protocols prevented nascent agrarian communities from engaging in ruinous wars, yet ensured that their respective farmers would fight and so keep a tight rein on political power, which meant few taxes for capital expenditure other than for agriculture. In short, the early Greek city state had found a mechanism to limit defence expenditure, keep religion apart from both war and politics, and make military policy hinge on the majority vote of the citizens – all that saved lives, property and money. If hoplite fighting appeared absurd – decisive battle without extensive fatalities, the choice of level battlefields rather than defensible mountain passes, heavy bronze armament under the Mediterranean sun, the diminution of both the poor and the very wealthy – at least it worked for a purpose; the preservation and expansion of an agrarian middle class.

Scholars often underplay the agrarian basis of early Greek warfare, but Greek literature abounds with this explicit connection between farming and fighting, emphasizing the rural genesis of hoplite warfare, the continual interplay between the two, and the revolutionary idea that warfare would serve the citizenry rather than vice versa. In contrast, sea power before the fifth century was rare. The late fourth-century Athenian *ephebes*, young warriors who took up the shield and spear to patrol the countryside, still swore in the twilight days of the *polis* quite formally to protect 'the wheat, the barley, the vines, the olives, and the figs'. The historian and soldier Xenophon always felt there was an intrinsic historical relationship between farming and the cohesion of the phalanx: 'Farming teaches one how to help others. For in fighting one's enemies, just as in working the soil, it is necessary to have the assistance of other people.'

Agricultural metaphor abounds in Greek military literature. The battle parlance of the Greek phalanx – 'horns' of 'yoked' men who 'threshed it out' – came from agriculture or rural life, not urban or maritime experience. Indeed, the word phalanx itself, denoting the ranks or stacks (*phalanges*) of heavy infantry in battle order, originally derived from the Greek for 'beam' or 'log', a logical assumption if most of its fighters lived in the country. Gruesome pitched battle between bloodstained men on foot was second nature between men who had killed game, slaughtered livestock and dug earth. It was this unique symbiosis between agriculture and warfare that explains why Greek authors often commented on the productive potential of farmland *not* in terms of soil, arability or mere size, but simply by the number of hoplite infantry a region might theoretically support. In early Greek eyes, the land alone produced soldiers. Soldiers alone came from the land.

Battlefields, then, were mostly unobstructed grainfields either close by the border itself or located in the path of obvious routes of invasion. Since phalanxes stacked eight deep and more, battle lines even in the largest of hoplite engagements rarely ever stretched more than a mile or two, allowing armies to fit in even the smallest of plains. Naturally, we hear frequently of perennial 'hotspots' and 'chokepoints' where strife broke out generation after generation. A good example is the high upland plateau of Thryeatis between Argos and Laconia where the respective armies battled continuously for over two centuries. The Megarian and Corinthian boundaries were also predictable sources of combat between hoplite armies. And at least five Greek battles were fought in the narrows of the Mantinean plain in antiquity. More

Most Classical Greek battlefields were planted in wheat or barley, which the invaders attempted to harvest or burn to force the defenders to fight. Many such fields were slightly uneven or even hilly – Delium is a good example – despite Herodotus's description of the 'fairest and most level ground'.

notorious still were the feuds between Phocis and Locris over the highland of Mount Parnassus, and the rivalry of Elis and Arcadia over the Alphaeus valley near Olympia. These disputed strips were not necessarily prime real estate (though all land was increasingly valuable), but represented to agrarian communities the all-important idea of sacrosanct territoriality. Border encroachment was a blow to civic esteem, and might lead to further aggrandizement if not checked.

The great plain of Boeotia, with its narrow entries and exits, was the obvious collision point for hoplite armies descending from northern Greece and marching up from Attica or the Peloponnese; the Theban general Epaminondas rightly labelled it 'the dancing floor of war', a veritable Spartan, Athenian and Theban slaughterhouse over a 200-year period where at least ten major engagements were fought, all within a 20-mile radius of Thebes. Only a few miles separate the battles of Plataea (479), Tanagra (457), Oenophyta (457), Delium (424), Haliartus (395), Coronea (first 447; second 394), Tegyra (375), Leuctra (371) and Chaeronea (338).

In the Classical period, local contingents defending their own farms were always given the position of honour on the right wing of a coalition phalanx, superseding even the claims of those allies who had the greater reputation for prowess. The fourth-century orator Demosthenes noted with nostalgia that warfare of the original *polis* had been a more moral enterprise, limited to summer campaigning among amateur militias. Plato, in his *Republic*, argued that normal Greek practices were still too harsh and advocated refinements that further mitigated the carnage wrought by Greeks against one another. Ancient treaties among city states sometimes outlawed both missile weapons and precluded any opportunity for pursuit after the main engagement.

Most major hoplite battlefields reflected the geographical and economic realities of the Greek mainland, as these examples of the more important engagements attest. The scene of infantry fighting tended to occur near more populated regions with good farmland and easy access to the coast, and along the major north-to-south routes of transit through central Greece.

Greek Battles, 700 – 168 BC

Greek States

1. Lelantine, 700 BC
2. Hysiae, 669 BC
3. Marathon, 490 BC
4. Thermopylae, 480 BC
5. Salamis, 480 BC
6. Plataea, 479 BC
7. Mycale, 479 BC
8. Oenophyta, 457 BC
9. Tanagra, 457 BC
10. Coronea, 447 BC, 394 BC
11. Pylos, 425 BC
12. Delium, 424 BC
13. Mantinea, 418 BC, 362 BC
14. Decelea, 413 BC
15. Arginusae, 406 BC
16. Aegospotami, 404 BC
17. Haliartus, 395 BC
18. Nemea, 394 BC
19. Corinth, 390 BC
20. Tegyra, 375 BC
21. Leuctra, 371 BC
22. Cynoscephalae, 364 BC
23. Chaeronea, 338 BC
24. Granicus, 334 BC
25. Sellasia, 221 BC
26. Pydna, 168 BC

Such military rituals tied to agriculture usually did not apply to war against foreign opponents and were not always adhered to by the Greeks themselves. But among the phalanxes of the city states at least there were a few clearly defined 'rules' of fighting – the so-called *nomima* of the Greeks – that were often in force for most of the seventh and sixth centuries, and sometimes still followed even during the hoplite decline in the fifth and fourth centuries:

1. Formal declaration of war and explicit abrogation of existing truces and treaties. There were few surprise infantry attacks or undeclared wars before the mid fifth century when a legal framework arose to define and circumscribe war (*polemos*), peace (*eirêne*), and shades of hostility in between. Both sides marched forward under the assumption – often formalized by their leaders – that theirs was a just, lawful and noble war.

2. Pre-battle ritual and shock collision between phalanxes. Formal notification of battle, public sacrifice of a domesticated animal before the ranks to sanction attack, and a brief harangue by the battlefield commander – all anticipated the charge of columns and collision of armies.

3. Fighting during spring and summer and limited to daylight hours. Flat terrain, not mountain passes or hillsides, was by agreement the locus of engagement. Night attacks were rare if not non-existent. Campaigning was not year-round.

4. Cessation of killing. Pursuit of the defeated was limited by both time and space; twilight marked the end to killing, and the mountains a refuge for the defeated. The wounded hoplites were not finished off; neither were prisoners executed. The captured enemy instead was either freed or given the chance of ransom before being enslaved.

5. Postmortem accord. Battle dead were not to be mutilated but returned under truce or formal treaty, which led to a recognized sense of legal capitulation. The beaten side formally requested the return of its fallen, which thus sanctioned its own defeat; and the victorious army constructed a public trophy on the battlefield, which was not to be contested or defaced.

6. Confinement of fighting. Heralds and citizens were usually spared. So, too, sanctuaries, temples and Panhellenic religious sites were to be exempt from infantry attack or occupation.

7. Limitations on technology. Battle was decided by spear and shield, powered by muscular strength and governed by sheer nerve. Eligibility for infantry service was based originally on agricultural production, which explained census classes. Wealthier auxiliary cavalry and poorer light-armed troops were confined to occasional pre-battle and post-battle skirmishing – even in Classical Athens horsemen made up only 5 per cent of the adult citizenry eligible for military service. In addition, landless archers, slingers and stone throwers were either absent altogether or relegated to the margins of the battlefield. Sophisticated artillery and siege engines – the wages of taxation and an urban professional class – were mostly phenomena of the fourth century and later.

In early hoplite warfare, then, there were rules and a predictable sequence of action which governed even the aftermath of battle. Similarly there was also a widespread civic consciousness of the ultimate sacrifice of the citizens who fought. Funeral orations (*epitaphoi*) were public events. Corpses were normally collected, identified and buried. Often casualty lists – like the American memorial in Washington, DC, to those lost in Indochina – were erected for public display, and the soldiers listed sequentially by the year in which they were killed. Private graves were adorned with moving representations of the dead at their most heroic moments in battle; major highways were sometimes lined with grave steles and battle monuments. Even the smallest of the city states – Thespiae in Boeotia is a good example – might produce an entire array of incised hoplite grave steles, which remain unmatched as examples of the best of the Greek plastic arts. Temple frieze courses and ceramic vases mirrored the general themes of epic and lyric poetry: the noblest sacrifice was to die in infantry battle, which assured an honoured spot in the underworld. Pericles said a glorious death in battle for the fatherland wiped clean at one stroke all previous flaws in a man's life. Ancient historians in their battle accounts often note by name those prominent citizens killed, and it is no surprise that we hear of some of the most famous – and infamous – in Greek history who perished in the ranks – King Leonidas of Sparta, the poet Archilochus, the brother of Aeschylus, the Athenian demagogue Cleon, the brilliant Spartan strategists Lysander and Brasidas, and the noble Boeotian statesmen Epaminondas and Pelopidas. The philosopher Socrates and the orator Demosthenes were only a few of the notable hoplites who escaped death by inches.

Yet, for all the hoplite monopoly of Greek warfare, there were intrinsic paradoxes in such infantry military practice that would eventually undermine the entire system, causing the understood protocols to become increasingly irrelevant as warfare evolved beyond set infantry collisions. As the Greek city states prospered throughout the Aegean and Adriatic in the fifth and fourth centuries, substantial capital was created not only from agriculture but from maritime trade as well. This growing flexibility and expansion of the ancient economy had disastrous results for the general practice of Greek warfare as hoplite battle. Hoplite warfare had once worked not because of some conspiracy of middling farmers, but because it was a practical and effective way of protecting the agricultural property that was the exclusive lifeblood of the small *polis*. Once small property owners lost their economic – then soon their political – dominance within the city state, pitched battle became but one of many 'roads of war', and was free to evolve according to the market-place of western science, technology and materialism.

Moreover, the very practice of equating landholding with exclusive citizenship rights and military service was always tenuous, as holders of 10-acre plots never made up much more than half of the resident male population of the *polis*. Others – the landless poor, resident aliens, even the unfree – were intrinsically no less capable in war – if the theatre of Greek warfare ever migrated from the farmland around the *polis* to the sea, mountains and overseas territory where horsemen, archers and sailors were essential. And if radicalized democracy or sheer economic growth gave the landless clout, they surely would expect to fight for things other than farmland and to be paid well in the process.

One of the great paradoxes – and tragedies – of agrarian war, then, was that its rules of engagement which so checked the inherent dynamism of western warfare were themselves predicated on the arbitrary exclusion of half the adults who lived in a Greek city state. When particular Greek city states found ways to end the exclusive connection between yeomanry and battle, new opportunities, both political and military, arose for a previously neglected 'other' – bringing far higher casualties at a time when states became ever more democratic. As we shall see, one of the most unstable forces in the history of western warfare was also the most equal: the emergence of Athenian democracy – in which the wisdom and morality of fighting wars rested entirely with the collective mood of the citizenry on any given day of the Assembly – proved lethal for the rest of the Greek city states.

THE EMERGENCE OF ATHENIAN AND SPARTAN MILITARY POWER

By the end of the sixth century, with the decline of Corinthian, Samian and Argive tyrannies, both Athens and Sparta were emerging as the two premier city states on the Greek mainland. Both enjoyed an array of natural and cultural advantages that could be put to good military use. The territories around each were unusually large – Laconia covered over 2,000 square miles and Attica nearly 1,000 – and well populated by Greek standards. Both states were the nominal centres of their respective Dorian and Ionic cultures, and so assumed a natural leadership over the populous Doric states in the Peloponnese and the Ionic settlements in the Aegean and on the coast of Asia Minor. Each side could muster loyal allies for foreign campaigns.

Athens and Sparta both had relatively tranquil political leadership in the seventh and sixth centuries which fostered economic growth and social cohesion. At Sparta the so-called Great Rhetra of Lycurgus inaugurated a tripartite system of power-sharing among two kings, a council of elders, and a body of executive overseers that prevented insurrection and revolution, providing the cherished ideal of *eunomia* – 'good law'. Group messes, age-class groups, and regimentation that centred on the barracks also ensured that élite Spartiates (the *homoioi* or 'Similars') developed an unusual sense of egalitarianism, seeing themselves as an homogeneous body clearly defined and set apart from the far more numerous helots and other 'inferior' peoples of their surrounding territory. Rivalries and squabbling among the Similars, with potential for wider insurrection and civil strife among the warrior class, were kept to a minimum. The population of Laconia and nearby Messenia was considerable, but the numbers of Similars small – making egalitarianism among a small clique easier, but also ensuring manpower problems in the future for the Spartiate phalanx, which in its genesis was little more than an internal security force.

At Athens the reforms of Solon (*c.* 600) formalized the chauvinism of the emerging yeoman hoplite, ensuring him political representation free from aristocratic backlash and with clear perquisites not shared by the landless poor. Despite intervals with tyrannies – although even the strongman Peisistratus and his sons were relatively enlightened – Athens, like Sparta, enjoyed political stability that encouraged food production, trade, and population growth. Attica produced an effective and proud local army, quite able to keep most intruders outside her borders and to incorporate neighbouring territory and nearby islands. In the very year after Cleisthenes organized the democracy (507), Athenian forces defeated both Chalcis on the island of Euboea and the neighbouring Boeotians – a testament to the military cohesion and *élan* that could accrue from the new idea of *isonomia*, or 'equality of political rights'.

In entirely different ways both states also freed themselves from the repressive material, monetary and ethical constraints that agriculture put upon the practice of warfare. No Greek city state – not even the feudal fiefdom of Thessaly or the isolated towns of Crete – enslaved an entire neighbouring population the size of Messenia as Sparta did, and thus directed its energies not to farming but to military training to ensure free food. Athens too had, by the fifth century, turned increasingly to her navy, and ultimately collected tribute from her vassal states overseas, freeing her from the need to fight in synchronization with the grain harvest. If Attic farmers would not or could not pay taxes for a new brand of all-out war, the city state could simply expropriate the money from cowed allies. On several occasions during the fifth century Athens was even willing to evacuate Attica altogether in order to keep her population safe and her fleet intact and on patrol.

Yet Sparta and Athens, while alike in their liberation from most *polis* economic and military restrictions, were actually very different. Athens evolved into a dynamic, maritime city state eager for trade, with a sizeable number of resident aliens, and by the fifth century replete with a navy and impressive urban and port fortifications. She was also probably the first radical democracy in Greece, and soon took on the responsibility of extending the vote to the landless but free poor elsewhere. And Attica's population was huge by Greek standards – perhaps somewhere between a quarter and a third of a million people – and prosperous, with maritime employment, mining revenues, and over 200,000 acres of arable land. The enfranchisement of the landless doubled the size of the participatory citizenry, guaranteed rowers for a sizeable navy, and soon became in itself a constant impetus for overseas expansion and aggrandizement.

In the Athenian way of war, material goods and manpower were far more important than hoplite muscle. And the Greek world would learn that the unruly mercurial democracy was a lethal war-maker – Herodotus noted that it was easier to convince 30,000 to go to war at Athens than a single man at Sparta. In fact, more Greeks were killed fighting for or against Athens than in all the wars in the history of the Greek city state. Democracy, in the ancient context, acted as a spur, not a brake, to military aggression and war-making. And democratic practices abroad meant nothing at home when it was a question of Athenian self-interest – the Assembly might as readily fight to exterminate democracies like Syracuse (415–413) as to aid oligarchies like Sparta in their war against Epaminondas' efforts to end helot apartheid (370–362).

Sparta, on the other hand, had remained parochial and isolated, with a small navy, no walls, no monetary economy, and little desire to welcome foreigners into the sanctum of Laconia. Her conservatism was as legendary as was the liberality of Athens; strict regimentation by age and class meant a small population – the Spartan curse of *oliganthrôpia* – and it was rare for the Spartiates to number much more than 10,000 warrior citizens. Unlike Athens, her strategy was simple: keep the helots down, the Peloponnese free of northerners, and support oligarchies wherever possible. And while no army until Epaminondas' early fourth-century crusade entered Spartan ground, it was nearly as rare in the seventh and sixth centuries to see her hoplites marching north.

In the cases of both Athens and Sparta, slaves were critical to the practice of warmaking, albeit in radically different ways. Indeed, the rise of the free Greek city state itself is linked to the wide-scale introduction of chattel slavery – and large segments of Greek citizenry could obtain individual ownership of unfree labour with sanction and encouragement, not interference, from the state, thus finding an egalitarian solidarity through the recognition of their own superiority over an entire body of inferiors. Most servile workers were originally engaged in agriculture, so they naturally accompanied their yeoman masters to war, in which they played vital roles as baggage and weapons carriers, and could canvass the battlefield either dutifully to recover the corpses of their fallen owners, or in search of loot. The peculiar elements of hoplite warfare – as was true of intensive agriculture in the Greek manner – cannot be understood without servile attendants. The sheer weight of the equipment demanded slaves to transport an army even a short distance.

Yet two very distinct systems of slavery developed in Greece. Both involved agriculture and warfare; both explain in a large part the marked differences between Spartan and Athenian warmaking. In general, Athens, like most Greek city states, developed from a free society of small landowners, who formed militias and used chattels to work their small plots. But with the rise of an imperial culture in the fifth century, together with the wide-scale exploitation of silver mines at Laurium, Athens drew in an unusually large number of non-agricultural slaves to work in the building trades, the silver industry, and small-scale manufacture.

There may have been as many as 100,000 unfree workers in Attica at the outbreak of the Peloponnesian War (431), servile labourers who not only carried their masters' hoplite armour on campaigns, but were also occasionally mass-conscripted into the army and navy in times of extraordinary crisis, such as Marathon (490) or the sea-battles at Arginusae (406) and Aegospotami (404). And while Athenian slaves were of different races and dialects, attached to individual families, and thus less likely to revolt in mass, their rare flights in great numbers – such as their desertion from the defeated army at Sicily (413) or their retreat to the Spartan stronghold in Attica at Decelea (413–404) – seriously weakened both Athenian military and economic power. Ancient historians too often ignore their presence on the battlefield, but we should imagine that thousands of slaves were present in some capacity on land and sea at nearly every major Athenian confrontation. Again, Greek warfare as it was practised was simply impossible without slaves, even if nearly all of these anonymous warriors are lost to the historical record.

Sparta, in contrast, sought to solve her problems of growing population and finite land not by intensive servile labour in agriculture and small crafts, but by annexing, in the eighth and seventh centuries, the entire territory and people of Laconia and neighbouring Messenia – perhaps a combined population of 250,000 – in a series of brutal wars and insurrections that lasted nearly three centuries. These indigenous populations were not simply enslaved to be sold off piecemeal or claimed by individual Spartan farmers. Instead, the Spartans kept them working *en masse* on their ancestral plots as serfs, owned by the state, not private individuals. These second- and third-class residents – the term *heilôtai* may have been derived from 'those taken' – contributed large portions of their agricultural produce to the communal messes of the Spartan warriors. Their treatment was therefore often harsher than chattels elsewhere in the Greek city states, as entire communities, not mere individuals, were relegated to inferior status, obviating all chance of close paternal relationship between warrior and personal attendant.

Helots represented a real and constant threat to Spartan culture. Such serfs lived and worked together; their linguistic and ethnic cohesion raised the constant spectre of insurrection and rebellion, and helps explain in large part the militaristic nature of Spartan society itself. Sparta evolved into an élite colony of warriors who did not farm, but as state police constantly trained for war, foreign and domestic, each year ritualistically declaring war on their own enslaved. No wonder that Sparta alone of the city states felt the need for a Gestapo-like secret police (*krypteia*).

It is not difficult, then, to understand the growing chasm between Athenian and Spartan approaches to warfare. Their mutual deviance from the standard practice of insular agrarian warfare gave both enormous military advantages over the parochial hoplites of most of the other rural-based 1,000 city states – superior capital and manpower in the case of the former, unrivaled infantry professionalism and training for the latter. If Athens increasingly evolved into an 'anti-hoplite' power, then Sparta regressed into a 'hyper-hoplite' state. By the fifth century 'Athenian' and 'Spartan' were synonymous not merely with different ways of fighting but with an antithesis at the heart of Greek culture itself. 'We trust less in system and policy than in the native spirit of our citizens. In education, where our rivals from their very cradles seek after manliness through painful discipline, we at Athens live exactly as we please.' So Pericles bragged in his famous funeral oration that Athenian liberality was always a match for Spartan militarism on and off the battlefield.

Was the Athenian general accurate about Spartan inherent weakness or simply playing to the nationalist chauvinism of his Athenian listeners? The reputation of the 'Dorian Spear' – earned largely during the Spartans' heroic last stand at Thermopylae (480) and through their granite-like resolve on the right wing at Plataea (479) – often sent terror through most opponents. At Pylos (425), for example, the Athenians trembled at the thought of facing the Spartiates. And in a speech of the orator Lysias, an Athenian veteran is simply quoted, 'It is a terrible thing to fight the Spartans'. And so often it was.

The mystique of Spartan militarism was deliberately amplified by a few macabre touches. Spartan soldiers marched in ostentatious red cloaks – supposedly to mask blood. They wore their hair long and oily, their helmet crests occasionally (at least for officers) turned transverse, in the style of Napoleon. Their onslaught was deliberately slow, at a walk accompanied to the sound of flutes. So Plutarch remarked that they 'marched in step to the pipe, leaving no confusion in their hearts, but calmly and cheerfully advancing into danger'. Greek literature is replete with stories of men who ran at the very sight of the Spartan phalanx, once they caught sight of their portentous *lamdas* – the Ls for Lacedaemon emblazoned on their shields.

Yet surprisingly, the Spartan infantry, for all its vaunted training and repute – like the latter-day German army – was not invincible.

They suffered numerous defeats – at Hysiae (669), Tegea (560), Thermopylae (480), Pylos (425), Haliartus (395), Lechaeum (390), Tegyra (375) and Leuctra (371) – from a variety of Greek and foreign armies. In all these cases, once they marched out of the vale of Laconia, the Spartan army was often tentative and unsure of its mission – a conservatism and paranoia at the very heart of their brutal system of apartheid. At Mantinea (418) and Leuctra (371), for example, only with reluctance did the Spartans settle on pitched battle. Often – for instance, at Marathon and during many of the seasons of the first decade of the Peloponnesian war – they stayed home, begging off on account of religious observances, earthquakes, reluctant allies, or worries over domestic insurrection.

In contrast, the Athenians with capital and men at their disposal, and a frenzied crowd in the Assembly, as Pericles put it, 'forced every sea and land to be the highway of our daring'. They routinely – and often recklessly – sent their democratic armies throughout Greece and the Mediterranean, undaunted when their hoplites or rowers perished *en masse* – thousands never came home from an ill-advised Egyptian campaign during the early 450s – ever eager, in a way undreamed of by Sparta, to empty the city once again in the hope of foreign aggrandizement through victory at sea and on the battlefield. In the year 459, a public casualty list for a single tribe at Athens lists soldiers killed fighting in Cyprus, Egypt, Phoenicia, Aegina, Megara, and in the Argolid – that is, Athenian hoplites and sailors were simultaneously on campaign or fighting 800 miles away in northern Africa, nearly 1,000 miles distant in Asia Minor, on the Greek mainland and in the Aegean. In short, if at Sparta the confining tactics of the conservative hoplite phalanx dictated strategy itself, at Athens the reverse was true: Mediterranean strategic ambition demanded tactical variety and experimentation.

Understandably, Thucydides believed that Syracuse, itself an enormous democratic city state, with numerous allies and a large navy – like Athens in so many ways – gave Athens much trouble: the danger for a reckless, large and rich democracy was another reckless, large and rich democracy. In set hoplite battles, especially within the Peloponnese, the well-drilled Spartans were usually invincible. But should the theatre of operations widen, the cosmopolitan and free-thinking nature of Athenian democratic society made its soldiers far more adaptable and audacious – precisely those traits which were needed both to acquire and to lose an empire.

So Sparta and Athens each developed along idiosyncratic but separate paths, for much of the seventh and sixth centuries neither overtly hostile nor especially friendly to one another. Unfortunately, the Persian invasion of Greece brought their armies together – at first into concerted defence of Greece, and eventually into a growing, bitter and inevitable rivalry. It was not the ruin of the Peloponnesian war (431–404) that doomed the old city state and its parochial practice of hoplite warfare, but rather its very success against Persia half a century earlier, a victory that showed all Greeks that they could prosper, fight and conquer far better than others in the Mediterranean – and do so far removed from the military and social constraints of the old agrarian *polis*. And no two *poleis* emerged, after the dramatic victory over Persia, more powerful, more prestigious and more unlike the other city states than Sparta and Athens, who now knew – and feared – each other so well.

CHAPTER THREE

The Great Wars (490–362)

This early marble bust, which was found on the Spartan acropolis, is often associated with Leonidas, the heroic Spartan king who courageously chose to die, with 299 of his royal guard, at Thermopylae in 480. In fact, while the sculpture may represent another early Spartan hero or god, the stern expression of resolve, elegant though simple headgear, and muscular physique magnificently capture the Spartan ideal.

The defence of Greece

A T THE BEGINNING OF the fifth century, Athens and the city state of Eretria on the large island of Euboea lent support to the Greek states on the western coast of Asia Minor who planned to rebel against their Persian overseers. The so-called Ionian revolt (499–494) was at first surprisingly successful for a non-imperial people who rarely unified for any group enterprise other than Panhellenic festivals and games, and had little logistical experience in transporting hoplite armies over large distances.

The combined Greek forces marched inland and burned the Persians' western capital at Sardis in 498. But as happened so often in both ancient and modern Greek incursions eastward into Asia Minor, further reinforcements were not forthcoming from the distant Greek mainland, logistical problems in Asia arose, and the momentum was lost. Ionia was a wealthy country in its own right, and rarely in Greek history warranted much more than sympathy from the more rugged Greeks to the west, who often equated temperate climates and rich soils with poor infantry and an absence of warlike spirit. Within five years of the revolution's outbreak Darius I, the Persian king, defeated the Greek fleet at Lade, captured the Greek coastal city of Miletus in 494, and sought revenge against the principals involved.

Although the historian Herodotus claims that Darius and the Persian court knew little about the Greek city states across the Aegean, it is more likely that for decades they presented a much sought-after prize. Hellenic interference in Persian imperial affairs now gave the king clear justification for retaliation. The prior destruction of Greek land and sea forces during the Ionian revolt also made the invasion seem militarily feasible.

So in 491 Darius began organizing a fleet to cross the Aegean, and sent emissaries to the island states requesting obeisance. On the eastern mainland, Eretria and Athens, prominent parties to the failed rebellion in Ionia, were logically the first targets of retribution on or near the mainland. After their fall, it seemed likely that most of the northern and eastern mainland Greek states might be bullied into some subordinate

Archers in Greece were held in disdain, but not so in Persia, where they were among the most esteemed and effective of the King's soldiers. Their arrows, though, had little effect at Marathon.

relationship without a great deal of campaigning or even much of a constabulary force, the entire Greek peninsula finally finding its proper role as the western-most satrapy of the empire.

The Persian onslaught in Greece proper began favourably, with the siege, capitulation and destruction of Eretria. Across the channel on the north-west coast of Attica, the small bay at Marathon was the nearest suitable landing on the mainland. It was relatively flat ground for cavalry and good autumn pasture land; it offered easy access to Athens herself; and it was a convenient gathering point for anti-democratic provocateurs who lived in the surrounding environs. The Persian army of between 20,000 and 30,000 landed there unopposed, and presumably made ready for a march across the mountains to give the Athenians the same treatment as the unfortunate Eretrians.

But the Athenians and their seventeen-year-old democratic culture were no Eretrians. Almost immediately they were on the march north under the leadership of Miltiades and Callimachus, the most prominent of the elected generals, at the head of nearly 10,000 Athenian hoplites, joined only by about 1,000 infantry from tiny Plataea. Once they arrived at Marathon several days of delay followed, as the democratic Athenian leadership on the battlefield debated the wisdom of attacking a force three times its size, with no reinforcements from the other Greek city states on the horizon.

THE WARS OF THE ANCIENT GREEKS

| 1 |
GREEK STATES
area *c.* 40,000 sq miles
103,000 sq km
population *c.* 1,000,000

| 2 |
PERSIAN EMPIRE
area *c.* 2,900,000 sq miles
7,511,000 sq km
population *c.* 20,000,000

**The Greek states and
the Persian empire,** *c.* 486 BC
■ Greek states
■ Persian empire under Darius

Istrus

Phanagoria

Odessus

Skudra

Black Sea

Apollonia

Pella

Byzantium

Sinope

Phasis

**Tyaily
Drayahya**

Trapezus

Sparta

Athens

Sardes

Sparda

Katpatuka

Ionia

Karka

R. Tigris

Tarsus

Arbela

Antioch

Athura

**Abr
Nahir**

R. Euphrates

Mediterranean Sea

P   E

Barca   Cyrene

Opsis

Putaya

Babirush

Jerusalem
Gaza

Babylon

Memphis

Arabaya

Mudraya

R. Nile

N

0   200 km
0   200 miles

Red Sea

Tropic of Cancer

Rarely in the history of war has such a large imperial power failed to subdue an inferior immediate neighbour. The Persian empire had manpower reserves twenty to fifty times larger than Greece, and controlled a territory nearly seventy times as vast.

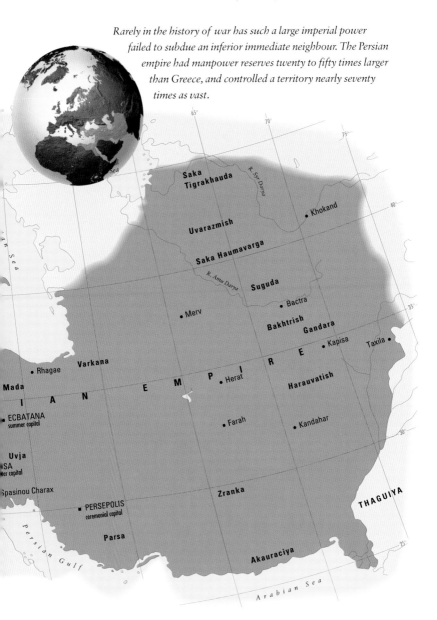

Saka Tigrakhauda

R. Syr Darya

Khokand

Uvarazmish

Saka Haumavarga

R. Amu Darya

Suguda

Bactra

Merv

Bakhtrish

Gandara

Kapisa

Taxila

Varkana

Rhagae

Mada

Harauvatish

Herat

ECBATANA
summer capital

Farah

Kandahar

Uvja

NSA
ter capital

Spasinou Charax

Zranka

THAGUIYA

PERSEPOLIS
ceremonial capital

Parsa

Persian Gulf

Akauraciya

Arabian Sea

In the end, however, as the Persians themselves gave signs of imminent attack, Miltiades persuaded his troops to take the initiative and the Athenians charged headlong into the Persians. While their own weakened center collapsed under the Persian weight, the two Greek wings broke through the Persian lines, rolled up behind the enemy, and forced both the defeated and victorious Persian troops back to their ships, killing 6,400 of them in the process. Only 192 Athenians, and a lesser number of Plataeans, perished, together with their servants – a startling fatality ratio of more than thirty to one, which emphasized what havoc armoured spearmen in column and on flat ground might accomplish. Such lopsided comparative losses would be characteristic of all future encounters between East and West for the next two centuries, from the mercenary Ten Thousand to Alexander the Great's phalangites, emphasizing the Greek superiority in shock battle by highly disciplined armoured men in close formation.

To cap off the day's killing, the tired Athenian hoplites then trekked *en masse* for eight hours over the pass to save their unprotected city from the retreating Persian fleet, displaying remarkable endurance and confidence, and so capturing for ever the collective imagination of the West. The Persian fleet departed east when the victorious hoplites returned unexpectedly at Athens. The first large hoplite battle against foreigners had been an unqualified success.

On a cup from Athens, probably painted shortly after the Persian defeat at Marathon, a Greek hoplite finishes off his Persian adversary. Fabric and leather protected Persian warriors from head to toe, but they offered little safety from the spear and sword attacks of the armoured Greek hoplite.

For the next two centuries no Greek phalanx would ever be pushed off the field of battle by Persian troops; no eastern commander would ever again attribute destructive madness, much less 'silliness', to charging Greek infantry – and no Greek *polis* would ever doubt the martial capability of democratic government. Military historians have sometimes characterized the small hoplite battles of the archaic Greeks as 'primitive' in comparison with Near Eastern traditions of enormous armies of archers, horsemen, chariots and foot-soldiers. But the verdict of Marathon proved that far from being rudimentary, the introduction of a true heavy infantry militia and shock battle was in fact a brilliant and a revolutionary idea.

The victory at Marathon quickly became emblematic proof of the entire dynamism of western warfare – and testimony to the peculiar propaganda, advertisement and hype that only a free and highly individualistic society might produce. Aeschylus' brother died heroically on the beach grasping at the retreating Persian prows, his playwright sibling not far behind. Aristides, Miltiades and Themistocles, the pantheon of early democratic Athenian statesmen, all gained their later political capital at this battle. The tomb of the 192 fallen Athenians, the Plataeans' sepulchre, the Athenian victory trophy and the monument to the Athenian battle heroes became instant tourist attractions. Within thirty years a grandiose panorama of the battle was painted on the walls of the Royal Stoa in the Athenian agora. A half century later, Herodotus could still find inexhaustible stories: the Athenians had dashed a mile in their armour to meet the Persians; they were the first of the Greeks to endure the sight of the Medes; Pheidippides had run all the way to Sparta to fetch help and had met Pan on the way; a huge hoplite spectre appeared during the battle, blinding Epizelos the Athenian and killing the man at his side. And nearly eighty years after the battle, the chorus of Aristophanes' *Wasps*, the elder 'Marathon Men', sang of how they had run through the arrows to reach the Persians and shoved them back until evening. Even several centuries later the topographer Pausanias recorded that a visitor to Marathon might still hear the whinnying of Persian horses and see the marks of the tent of the Persian general Artaphernes.

We moderns are no better. Two and a half millennia later, the 26-mile 'Marathon' commemorates the Athenian march back to Athens to beat the Persian fleet and stop their embarkation. Miltiades' helmet sits in a glass case in the museum at Olympia. On any given day at Marathon

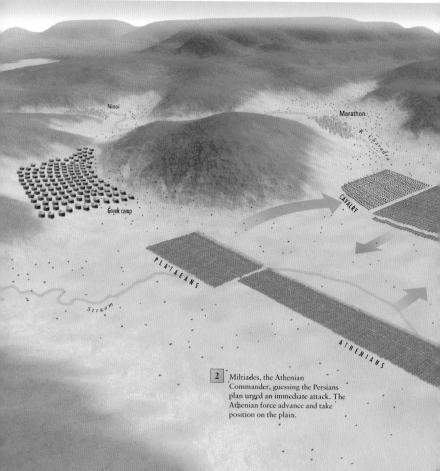

Ninoi

Marathon

R. Charadra

CAVALRY

Greek camp

PLATAEANS

Stream

ATHENIANS

2 | Miltiades, the Athenian Commander, guessing the Persians plan urged an immediate attack. The Athenian force advance and take position on the plain.

The Battle of Marathon

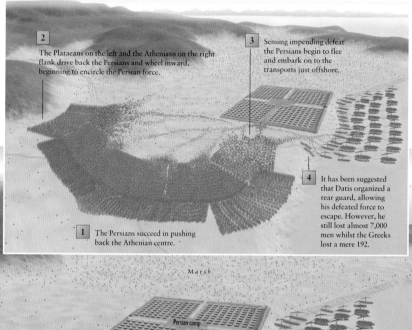

2 The Plataeans on the left and the Athenians on the right flank drive back the Persians and wheel inward, beginning to encircle the Persian force.

3 Sensing impending defeat the Persians begin to flee and embark on to the transports just offshore.

4 It has been suggested that Datis organized a rear guard, allowing his defeated force to escape. However, he still lost almost 7,000 men whilst the Greeks lost a mere 192.

1 The Persians succeed in pushing back the Athenian centre.

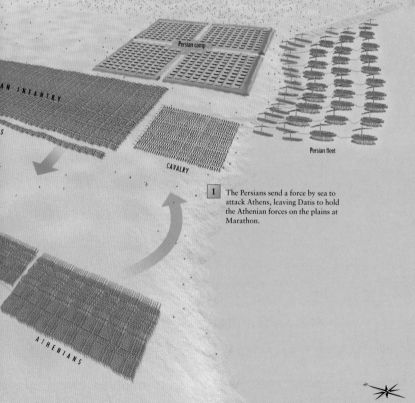

Marsh

Persian camp

AN INFANTRY

S

CAVALRY

Persian fleet

1 The Persians send a force by sea to attack Athens, leaving Datis to hold the Athenian forces on the plains at Marathon.

ATHENIANS

tourists with maps can be seen strolling around the modern museum and beach. The dynamism of western warfare was not found merely on the field of battle but extended even to *post bellum* imaginative re-creation and celebration – a monopoly on the presentation of history that still so infuriates western adversaries.

The victory at Marathon aborted only the first Persian invasion of Greece under Darius – a punitive incursion as it turned out, not a serious grand army of occupation as would come a decade later. The number of enemy combatants was not unduly impressive, less than 30,000. The defeated Persian army retreated to its ships and was not annihilated as it was later at Plataea (479). Nor was there even a Panhellenic consensus to stand down the invader at Marathon. Sparta's premier but superstitious hoplites conveniently stayed at home, purportedly waiting for the full moon before they could safely march out. They arrived only after the fight, and took a sightseeing tour of the battlefield to gaze at the Athenians' spear work. Fortunately for the Athenians, the failure of the Persians to use their cavalry wisely, if at all, the natural advantages which accrue to defensive troops against sea-borne invaders, and the confusion in Persian strategy, made up for the absence of Greek allies.

True, Greeks had fought Persians earlier in Ionia. But never had the two armies clashed in a single pitched battle, an occasion that might clarify and contrast two entirely antithetical military and political traditions: cavalry, archery and light-armed troops versus heavy infantry; coerced subjects against free militia; wealthy imperial invaders turned away by pedestrian defenders of farm and family. And unlike earlier, critical Greek battles like Hysiae (669), or Sepeia (494), we have a relatively full account of Marathon – indeed, Herodotus' colourful narrative is the first historical chronicle in prose of a large pitched engagement in European history. But more importantly, unlike the other fighting of the subsequent war with Xerxes, Marathon was a purely Athenian business and so warranted the entire focus of fifth-century Athenian literary, artistic and philosophical creativity and advertisement. It was soon enshrined as the last hurrah before the rise of Athenian maritime imperialism, when doughty farmers of Athens had stood alone against the world. Yet for later reactionary politicians and élite thinkers, Marathon was cast as the last good war of the city's last good generation before the contagion of sailors, foreigners and radical democrats took over and ruined the state.

But for all Greeks, the war with Persia was quickly envisioned as an ideological struggle between an oppressive, hubristic eastern power that shanghaied serfs into its massive armies, versus outnumbered yeoman citizens who might vote freely on their own accord to fight and preserve their liberty. The former preferred battle at a distance, the latter opted for brawling face-to-face. Whatever the accuracy of the Greek propaganda and such a simplistic antithesis, the Greeks' other observations about the technology and *élan* of the respective troops rang true: the war would pit large numbers of lightly armed bowmen, missile troops, poorly protected infantry and skirmishers against bronze-armoured hoplites who preferred to kill in shock battle. Whenever the Persians repeated the mistake of Marathon, and thus nullified their numerical superiority through the choice of battle in small plains or harbours, the Greek advantage in discipline, morale and technology on every occasion proved decisive.

Darius died in 486, and the task of avenging both the burning of Sardis and the shame of Marathon now fell to his son Xerxes. The latter was not intent on another punitive raid, but now envisioned a mass invasion, one larger than any the eastern Mediterranean had yet seen. After four years of preparation, in 480 Xerxes was ready. He bridged the Hellespont into Europe and descended through northern Greece, absorbing all the city states in his wake, unfortunate communities that had little choice but to surrender or be destroyed. While there is no credibility in ancient accounts that the Persian army numbered more than a million men, we should imagine that a force of even a quarter to half a million infantry and seamen was the largest invasion that Europe would witness until the Allied armada on D-Day. Neither do we need to agree with ancient accounts that the Persian cavalry numbered over 80,000 horse. But it may well have been half that size, still nearly five times larger than the mounted forces that Alexander would use to conquer Asia more than a century and a half later. To the Persians, the real trick was just in assembling such a horde and getting it into Greece intact. In comparison to that logistical nightmare – the Persian army was perhaps three times larger than Sherman's entire federal force that cut a 60-mile swath through Georgia on its march to the sea – the destruction of Greek military forces was felt to be relatively simple.

After heated discussions and several aborted efforts – the bellicosity of respective city states often depended on their proximity to the invasion route of Xerxes – the Greeks agreed to stop the onslaught at the narrow defile of Thermopylae, the last pass in Greece above the isthmus of Corinth where terrain offered a credible defence for outnumbered troops. At the chokepoint there was a passage of less than 50 feet (15 m) between the cliffs and the sea. Accordingly in August 480 the city states sent the Greek fleet under Athenian leadership up the nearby coast to Artemisium. King Leonidas of Sparta followed by land with a token allied force of less than 7,000 hoplites. If the Persian fleet could be stalled and the massive army bottled up, all the city states to the south might yet rally northward, join Leonidas, and so thwart the advance without much harm to the rich interior of central and southern Greece.

At first, events favoured the Greeks – despite the fleet being outnumbered by four to one, and the army by more than fifty to one. Leonidas stopped cold all Persian ventures into the pass, as a torrential storm wrecked 200 of the Persian ships off the coast between the mainland and the island of Euboea. On the second day of the Greek occupation of Thermopylae, Xerxes' formidable corps of Immortals was sent down the funnel, but fared no better against Leonidas. Meanwhile, additional Greek ships helped the allied fleet off the coast sink most of Xerxes' Cilician contingent. The Greeks were inflicting terrible casualties on the Persians with few losses to themselves, and gaining valuable time and psychological capital for the wavering city states to their rear. But even with horrific numbers of losses, the Persian fleet still totalled well over 600 ships, and the land army outnumbered Leonidas' by thousands.

By day three, an extraordinary moment in the history of Greek warfare, the Anopaia path to Leonidas' rear was betrayed to the Persians, and they now prepared an attack on the pass from both front and back – the Gauls (279) and Romans (191) would later use the same 'secret' route to overwhelm Greek defenders. To save his army and buy some time for the communities to the south, Leonidas sent away all but his 299 Spartiates and a small, brave, and doomed contingent from the Boeotian town of Thespiae. A few Thebans may have also volunteered – or been coerced – to stay behind. The Greeks now lumbered out recklessly to meet the Persians at the widest expanse, fighting until their weapons were ruined, their king slain, and the 299 Spartans and their friends slaughtered to the last man under a sea of arrows. From Herodotus' account and his anecdotes concerning bravery in the face of certain death, the Spartans on their final day appear no longer intent merely on the doomed fight for Thermopylae, but on the greater war for the hearts and minds of their more timid kindred to the south. In any case, they were unable to hold off the Persians, or to co-ordinate further resistance on land.

At the same time, the Greek fleet of 300 ships, under pressure, also slowly withdrew from the straits of Euboea. The way to Greece was wide open at last, but the martyrs of Thermopylae had proved that Greek courage and discipline might prevail, if Persian numerical superiority could somehow be neutralized through either wise generalship or Persian folly. In the Greek mind, the Spartan king – who was mutilated and decapitated – had not been beaten but betrayed.

Nearly all of the plains of Boeotia now lay open and its towns had little choice but to 'Medize', or join the Persians – a stain on Thebes that did not enhance the military reputation of conservative agrarian states, and one not wiped clean until the Theban heroic stand against Philip at Chaeronea a century and a half later. The victorious Persian army swept southward and in little more than a week entered an evacuated and nearly deserted Attica. In a historic decision with equally lasting ramifications for the next 150 years, the Athenians – without reliable fortifications around their

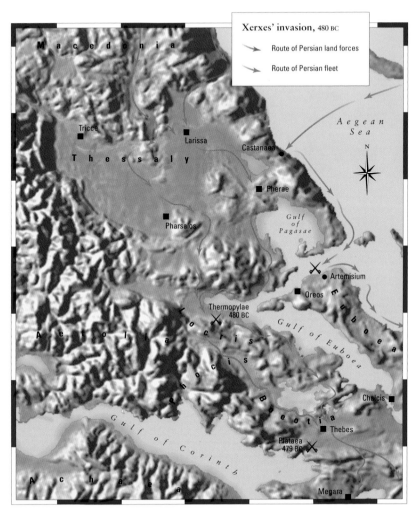

The terrain of Greece favoured the defenders. Passes in northern Thessaly, and at Thermopylae, together with narrow entries into Boeotia and along the Attic border, could be garrisoned or blocked by hoplites. The sea-coast from the Gulf of Pagasae to Salamis was irregular, replete with inlets and island channels that favoured harbour defence. And the mountains of western Greece made that region nearly impassable.

capital – deserted their city and put their faith solely in Themistocles and the navy. For decades afterwards, they would chauvinistically remind their fellow Greeks that they had handed over their ancestral homes to the torch in the defence of Hellenic freedom. In reality, they had little choice. Indeed, through such abandonment of the countryside and reliance on the fleet, Athens had now hit upon the formula for radical democratic imperialism that would exempt her from the consequences of hoplite battle and make her triremes and tax-collecting bureaucrats the bother of the Aegean for the next half century. Unlike the poor Thebans, the Athenians at least had a navy and easy refuge nearby.

Tentative contingents of the allied Greek fleet were congregated nearby at Salamis, pondering whether to sail south to the isthmus of Corinth and abandon the apparently lost cause to reclaim Athens. Yet the Greek admirals were persuaded by Themistocles to stay – otherwise, he threatened to have the Athenians refound their city elsewhere and leave the coalition entirely. In the eleventh hour of desperation, Attic farmers left their plots and paddled over to help man triremes. The era of hoplite supremacy and agrarian chauvinism at Athens – purportedly reaffirmed by the gallant run at Marathon a decade earlier – was now eroding in the face of an entirely new and total warfare. The defence of Greece rested mostly with the poor, who were the majority of the rowers of the Greek fleet and now alone could win back the city.

But for the first time in nearly two decades the Persians were to encounter the full force of a united Greece on both land and sea, led by Sparta and Athens, with thousands of crack hoplites and courageous sailors not inferior to those who had blocked the pass at Thermopylae. Under Themistocles' clairvoyant leadership, the Greeks were convinced to fight as a united fleet in the narrow channels off Salamis rather than retreating to save the Peloponnese at the isthmus. In the narrows between Attica and the island of Salamis, the Persians could not take full advantage of their overwhelming numerical superiority – perhaps 1,200 ships arrayed against the Greeks' 368 – and there was less chance that the Greek alliance might splinter and lose cohesion should battle be postponed.

Moreover, the Greek ships were probably less elegant, higher decked, and of stouter construction. In confined waters where manoeuvring was difficult, they could box in, target, and then ram the compressed Persian armada of varying nationalities, as hoplites speared survivors who were washed up on the shore. Once the Athenians succeeded in drawing the entire enemy fleet up into the strait between Salamis and the mainland – both the entrance and exit were narrow and full of Greek ships – the Persians, without much room for movement, became trapped. The battle commenced in late September 480 and resulted in a lopsided Greek victory, with the Athenians and Aeginetans playing the most prominent roles. Repeated ramming, confusion and panic among the Persian ships, and the desperate courage of the invaded – the Athenians had now lost their homes to the torch – resulted in 200 Persian ships being sunk and thousands of sailors being drowned. Less than forty Greek triremes were lost. Xerxes again watched from his throne on the heights; Themistocles, like Leonidas before him, fought with his men.

Few Greeks other than Themistocles had believed that ships alone might save the Greek city states. Navies were expensive and had no strategic importance before the fifth century. Most earlier fighting at sea was of a more private nature as pirates intercepted merchant vessels, stole their cargoes and enslaved their crews. The sixth-century Greek tyrant, Polycrates of Samos, was unique in creating a *thalassocracy* – or imperial rule based on an armada. But such forces were probably small and the ships crude. Because of agrarian protocol, warfare remained largely a land affair, and the trireme – the Greeks' fighting ship *par excellence* – was probably not even invented until the latter sixth century. Dockyard construction and ships could be funded only through foreign aggrandizement, and few states wished to invest capital on the strategy that they could acquire, maintain and plunder subjects across the water.

More importantly, social status was closely tied to military duty: those who owned a sufficient amount of farmland purchased their panoply, entered the phalanx, and sat in the governing council of the *polis*. Those who were poor or without land were either skirmishers or sought

Early Greek vase painting of the eighth and seventh centuries shows double-banked galleys or biremes, which might accommodate a total of 50–70 rowers. These early predecessors to the classical trireme, or three-banked ship, were originally developed by the Phoenicians, and served as the standard eastern Mediterranean warship until the late sixth century. We should assume that in wartime and national emergencies a large percentage of the crews was servile.

haphazard service at sea. Even the wealthy sometimes bragged that they had eschewed cavalry privilege, and fought instead on foot as hoplites, suggesting that infantry service brought more prestige than even membership in aristocratic cavalry.

If infantry service earned repute, rowing was confirmation of poverty, ignorance, and an inferior pedigree. Hoplite infantrymen brought their own arms and were suspicious of an all-powerful state; oarsmen wished for extensive ship and dock construction, and hence a large government that alone could raise the necessary revenue to keep the costly ships at sea. A hoplite put his own arms above the hearth, ready for battle at any moment; a sailor's oar and bench pad were worthless without a state ship. A hoplite wished to defend his community with a day of spear work; a rower with walls, taxes, and months of patrolling.

And the costs of sea power were exorbitant. A little more than 100 man-days of labour paid for a complete suit of armour and weapons; over 10,000 were needed to construct and outfit a single trireme. An army of 10,000 hoplites represented a capital investment of 200,000 drachmas in armour and slave attendants; yet a fleet of 100 ships and their rigging cost five times more, nearly a million drachmas. And while a hoplite army could march out, forage, fight, and be back in a week for not much more than 70,000 drachmas in infantry pay, a fleet of 100 triremes on patrol for a month might need twenty times more for salaries, upkeep and provisions.

Thus the need to fight the Persians at sea upset not merely the rules of Greek warfare, but also the social and economic equilibrium of the city state itself. The elevation of the navy – and its crews – to a coequal status ensured the increasing radicalization of Athenian democracy for the next half century. In the late 480s Themistocles had wisely convinced the Athenians to use their new-found mining revenues to build a fleet of 200 triremes, offering a maritime presence against future Persian sea-borne attack, and strategic justification for evacuating Attica in case of a massive Persian occupation.

But military strategy seldom operates in a vacuum. Themistocles was well aware that the promotion of naval service – well over 20,000 landless Athenian citizens may have rowed at Salamis – the sacrifice of the Athenian countryside, public financing of ship construction, and the accompanying diminution of the Athenian infantry, had considerable domestic ramifications: a landed and conservative minority could no longer claim monopoly on the city's defence. From now on, in all Athenian-led democracies, maritime power, urban fortifications, walls connecting port and citadel, and the employment of the poor on triremes were felt to be essential to the survival of popular governments, who would elect non-aristocrats like Themistocles – his mother was probably not even Greek – to guide the city. Taxes and forced contributions would pay for the investments. In times of national crisis the record of naval power at Artemesium and Salamis apparently confirmed that ships were strategically invaluable and their impoverished crews every bit as brave as hoplite landowners.

But to the agrarian conservative mind all this was anathema. All philosophers deplored the naval triumphs of the Persian wars and were frightened by the bellicosity of the rabble in the Athenian Assembly. Plato went so far as to say that the stunning naval victory at Salamis that saved western civilization made the Greeks 'worse' as a people, while Aristotle linked the sea-battles of the Persian wars with the rise of demagoguery itself. In their eyes, it was almost better to lose heroically on the hoplite battlefield than to win at sea with the help of an impoverished and poorly educated crowd, who would demand ever more entitlement and overseas booty to pay for it. Indeed, Aristotle felt that a city's military force could be reckoned only in the number of hoplites it fielded, the only troops virtuous enough to count as real warriors. History, however, was on the side of a more monetarized and market economy, foreign trade, and greater participation of the non-landed. The Persian challenge brought that truth home, demonstrating that, in the century to come, more than hoplites were needed to realize the new Greek political and economic ambitions in the Aegean and Mediterranean.

With the defeat of his fleet at Salamis, Xerxes retreated to his palace and harem, leaving his henchman Mardonius with an enormous land army in Attica, and orders to finish off the nearby Greek infantry before subduing the last remaining free city states south of the isthmus. True, the Greeks' first victory against the Persians now meant that they were safe from sea-borne attack to the rear, and the invaders were without naval support or the watchful eye of their dreaded king. But all of Greece from Athens northward was still in Persian hands, and there was an army of thousands that remained in the field to be annihilated.

The next summer the Hellenic alliance agreed to meet the army of Mardonius in Boeotia, and filed into the small town of Plataea, mustering the greatest army in the entire history of hoplite warfare, a force of at least 60,000 heavy infantry and perhaps an equal number of light-armed auxiliaries – even Alexander the Great never fielded forces

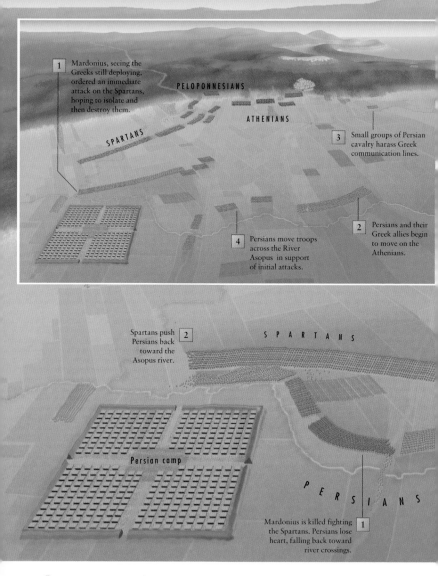

1 Mardonius, seeing the Greeks still deploying, ordered an immediate attack on the Spartans, hoping to isolate and then destroy them.

PELOPONNESIANS

ATHENIANS

SPARTANS

3 Small groups of Persian cavalry harass Greek communication lines.

4 Persians move troops across the River Asopus in support of initial attacks.

2 Persians and their Greek allies begin to move on the Athenians.

Spartans push Persians back toward the Asopus river. **2**

SPARTANS

Persian camp

P E R S I A N S

Mardonius is killed fighting the Spartans. Persians lose heart, falling back toward river crossings. **1**

PLATAEA

Once the Greeks had ensured that the battle would be decided between crack Spartan hoplites on the Greek right wing, and Persian horsemen under Mardonius, relative numbers and tactics no longer mattered much. The Persians had sought out the flat plain of Boeotia for their cavalry; in fact, it served as an ideal killing ground for the vast Greek army of hoplites – the largest Hellenic infantry force ever assembled in the

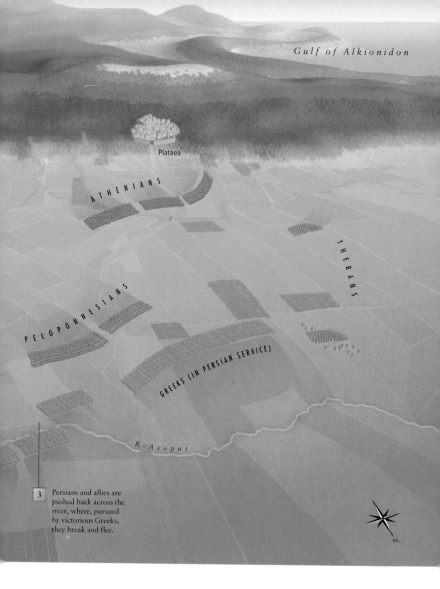

Gulf of Alkionidon

Plataea

ATHENIANS

THEBANS

PELOPONNESIANS

GREEKS (IN PERSIAN SERVICE)

R. Asopus

3 Persians and allies are pushed back across the river, where, pursued by victorious Greeks, they break and flee.

entire history of the city state. Once the Persians collapsed and Mardonius fell, the Medizing Greeks lost heart and the Athenians proved triumphant on the Greek left wing. Their excellence in siegecraft meant that the victors would go on to storm the Persian camp, and thus ensure that very few of the thousands of defeated invaders would ever return to Asia.

of such size. Yet the Greek hoplites were still outnumbered, and the army had no cavalry of the number or calibre to match Mardonius' horsemen – it was left to Philip II a century and a half later to develop heavy cavalry, armoured and equipped with a lance, to overwhelm eastern mounted archers and javelin-throwers. The allied commander, the Spartan regent Pausanias, was not about to expose his lumbering infantry in the wide plains of Boeotia, and sought instead to keep his army near the flanks of

By the fourth century the old economic, cultural and military disdain for horsemen was eroding in Greece as cavalrymen increasingly became objects of admiration. Such mounts as portrayed on this fourth-century marble stele alone might be valued at more than three complete suits of hoplite armour.

Mount Cithaeron, where reinforcements from throughout Greece poured in daily over the mountains, each man swearing formally, 'I shall fight to the death; I shall put freedom before life.'

Each side jockeyed for positions. Finally the Persians sent their cavalry against the Greek right wing, while the Medizing Boeotians attacked the Athenians over on the left. The Spartans and the nearby men of Tegea endured repeated cavalry and archery attacks, and then slowly went on the offensive, crashing into the enemy light infantry, destroying their left wing, killing Mardonius, and causing the entire Persian line to crumble and scatter to the north. Casualty ratios of thousands to a few hundred again revealed the superiority of hoplite infantry.

Scholars, ancient and modern, have faulted the tactical plan of Mardonius. In their view, he ignored the lessons of Marathon, foolishly entering a set battle against Greek heavy infantry, when the great plain of Boeotia gave an opportunity for hit-and-run attacks and for sudden sweeps of horsemen, which could pin the Greeks to the hills and slowly erode their fragile cohesion. Yet invaders far from home inevitably lose – as examples from Hannibal to the Americans in Vietnam attest – if they cannot force a decisive battle with the majority of forces of the invaded.

The difference in leadership between imperial Persians and elected Greek generals was also unmistakable: Achaemenid kings, who did not fight, erected marvellous tombs recounting their personal bravery in battle; Greek generals who battled in the phalanx were ridiculed, fined, censored or exiled should they attempt to claim any personal responsibility for victory.

The verdict of Plataea, and the subsequent Greek victory in Asia Minor at Mycale, brought a climactic end to the entire dream of eastern conquest in Europe. This was no accident. Plataea reflects a general – and inescapable – truth at the heart of the Persian dilemma: ultimately, the finest infantry in the world stood between their idea of conquest, and sooner or later thousands of Greek hoplites had to be faced, battled against, and killed off. The subsequent history of the city state confirmed there was not an army in the world anywhere that was up to the task.

THE PELOPONNESIAN WAR

In the aftermath of the Persian invasion and defeat, there was, as is common after any great social and cultural upheaval, a conscious return to normality in Greek warfare. Once more in military terms we hear for a time of a series of fifth-century hoplite 'wars' over borders among the Greek city states decided in the old way: traditional one-hour stand-offs between willing Greek city states at the battles of Dipaea (471), Tanagra and Oenophyta (457), and Coronea (447). But the Persian experience was not forgotten, as the lessons of the victories over Xerxes filtered slowly throughout Greek city states. Chief among the new realities were two phenomena that help explain the sharp break with *polis* warfare of the past.

First, the victory confirmed two city states, Sparta and Athens, as alone prestigious and pre-eminent – and both had demonstrated how abandoning agrarianism had brought real military dividends. The Spartan red-cloaks had anchored the entire Greek resistance at Thermopylae and Plataea, suggesting that their dreaded infantry would indeed venture outside Laconia and fight – if need be to the last man. Nor were the democratic Athenians comfortable with the status quo of war decided by the collision of amateur farmers. In the wake of the Persian withdrawal in 479, Athens' fleet only increased under Themistocles and a succession of gifted imperialists. Nurtured on the tribute of vassal states in the Aegean, Athenian triremes were not mothballed but became instead a 'benign' police force of sorts for her Greek subject allies overseas – between 200 and 300 were on near-constant patrol. Like the Spartans, imperial Athens too saw little need to limit warfare to a single afternoon border fight, or indeed, given the success of her evacuation before Xerxes and subsequent naval response, to risk her hoplites at all in defence of the farmland of Attica.

Second, the successful role of non-hoplite forces in the Persian wars had left a marked impression on the Greeks. Ships, light-armed troops and cavalry had all been present in a variety of theatres and terrains, underscoring how vulnerable and how inadequate the hoplite phalanx might become before any adversary who was not always willing to face it in a single land battle with heavy infantry. Yet the problem for the Greek *polis* was not merely fielding such diverse contingents, but rather coping with the invariable *social* challenges that accompanied the use of such forces. Give oarsmen, skirmishers or cavalry military importance, and the old agrarian exclusivity of the *polis* – the very fabric and ideology of the Greek culture itself – was challenged, as farmers with heavy armour and spears no longer warranted privileged social and political status.

Inevitably the half century after the end of the Persian wars saw the growth of the Athenian empire and the creation of satellite democratic subjects, which threatened the Peloponnesian alliance of Doric oligarchies who marched under Spartan leadership. Strategy now entailed more than border wars, since capital and power in the form of tribute, forced allied levies and expropriated farmland meant fielding all sorts of forces for weeks abroad.

Even maritime states like Corinth and Syracuse, as well as the agrarian yeomen of Thebes, were uneasy with the great fifty years of Athenian imperialism (479–431) and looked to the Spartan phalanx for balance. In their eyes the Athenians were not Pericles' 'school of Hellas', who had perfected Greek drama, built the Parthenon, and fashioned a dynamic culture based on overseas tribute, but rather an oppressive and unpredictable imperialist state, whose navy and democracy ensured turmoil for any who chose to stand in her way. After the defeat of Persia, most city states naïvely thought that Athens would relinquish its navy, remain unwalled, and return to its prior status as a powerful though fairly representative *polis*, albeit pre-eminent among equals, which would lead only in times of Panhellenic peril.

Instead, the victory over the Persians changed the entire political situation in Greece and inaugurated a radical transformation in western military thought and practice that would culminate a century and a half later with Alexander the Great poised at the Indus river. Throughout the decades following the Persian wars, most Greek states of the northern Aegean, Pontic region and coast of Asia Minor became tribute-paying Athenian dependencies. Any who resisted – Naxos, Thasos, Aegina,

Samos – were systematically besieged, slaughtered, or forced to pay indemnities. Athenian democracy, among other things, gained a notorious reputation for siegecraft: her ships could blockade any island in the Aegean, while skilled engineers built walls of circumvallation as her army disembarked to starve the enemy out. Recalcitrant subject states soon found their own insurrectionists executed, their wealthy classes exiled, and most of their land divided and handed over to the Athenian poor.

Few other states could afford the expense or had the expertise for resistance in this new brand of war – the nine-month successful siege of the island of Samos (440) cost possibly 1,200–1,400 talents, the equivalent to over eight million days of man labour, far more than the entire twenty-year tab for building the Parthenon. For the same outlay, nearly 3,000 Greek tragedies could have been produced at public expense. In fact, the subjugation of Samos alone cost the city more than all the Athenian plays – the tragedies of Aeschylus, Sophocles, Euripides, and dozens of others – produced in the entire fifth-century history of Attic drama. If we keep in mind the economy of the old style of agrarian warfare for the first two centuries of the city state (700–500), we can begin to understand how the rise of Athenian imperial democracy changed the entire practice – and balance sheet – of Hellenic warmaking.

For ten years (457–447) Athens had controlled Boeotia, while for sixteen years she policed the growing Corinthian fleet and kept Spartan influence confined to the Peloponnese during this so-called 'First' Peloponnesian war (461–446). In the eyes of the historian Thucydides, a conservative exiled Athenian admiral, democratic imperialism was a frightening juggernaut fueled by expropriated capital and the sheer numbers of the enfranchised poor, whose logical ambition was no less than the subjugation of Greece itself. Hence conflict between Athens and Sparta was inevitable, the sooner the better for the outclassed Peloponnesian allied states whose landed hoplite timocracies were at the mercy of the agricultural year and lacked the flexibility, manpower or money of a maritime democracy that grew continuously. The critical choice, as Sparta's allies saw it, was to march on Athens immediately or slowly die on the vine. And even then hoplite battle, as practiced by the Thebans and Spartans, did not ensure strategic success against the Athenians.

Unfortunately the great war between Athens and Sparta (431–404) was not decided in an afternoon. Instead the killing dragged on in various interludes and theaters for twenty-seven years. It is easy to see why. Sparta initially had neither the naval resources to dismantle the Athenian maritime empire, nor the logistical and technical skill to storm the walls of Athens. It had no capital to speak of, no mercenaries, ships or siege engineers, and since the mid sixth century relied exclusively on a large allied army of Peloponnesians who would only muster in the late spring before harvest.

Athens in turn was confronted by a novel two-front war, boxed in on the north by the Boeotians and on the south by the Peloponnesians. Both the latter states fielded superb infantry, so there was little chance that Athenian hoplites could successfully march into Thebes or Sparta, much less defeat an invading army in the Attic plain. This strategic dilemma – itself an entire rejection of the 300-year tradition of hoplite battle as the sole mode of war – quickly led all the belligerents to innovation and adaptation, and in the process unleashed as never before the Greek genius for technology and tactics. The subsequent barbaric siege and destruction of Plataea (431–427), the execution of civilians at Lesbos (427) and Scione (421), the incineration of the garrison at Delium (424) – a fantastic flame-thrower was employed in the siege – the butchery of schoolboys at Mycalessus (415) and the male citizens of Melos (415), the horrific fighting around Syracuse (415–413), and the continual raiding and plundering from Pylos (425) and Decelea (412–404) were all predicated on the use of ships, fortifications, skirmishers, slaves, ruse, night attacks, and technology, exploiting the hitherto untapped Greek ingenuity at killing outside the hoplite arena.

Both sides quickly learned of the 'terrible arithmetic' of war, understanding that hostilities might cease only when the prerequisite numbers of enemy soldiers were killed, the necessary number of civilians rendered homeless and hungry, and a sufficient amount of the national treasure exhausted. If the original hoplite renaissance marked the West's dramatic invention of decisive infantry confrontation and shock battle, the Peloponnesian war ushered in the complementary though far more horrific western idea of a total, absolute and just war, in which a free society's political, scientific and material resources were willingly and legally focused on annihilating the entire culture of the enemy. Before the Peloponnesian war, the massacre of civilians was extremely rare; once the war began it became commonplace – and none killed more freely than the imperial democracy at Athens.

The first phase, or so-called Archidamian war (431–421) – only much later did Thucydides and his contemporaries understand a more or less continuous struggle of twenty-seven years – saw the Peloponnesians enter Attica five times in the decade, hoping either to draw Athenian hoplites out to battle or to ruin the agriculture of Attica. Abandoning her countryside to Spartan invaders, Athens understandably refused pitched hoplite battle with the Spartan alliance, which was aided by both Boeotian infantry and cavalry from the north.

In the Periclean view, what had worked for Themistocles against the Persians might be even more successful against the unimaginative Spartans – especially since, after the Persian war, the erection of fortifications down to the port at Piraeus, the so-called Long Walls, meant that the city proper no longer had to be evacuated along with its countryside. The trick in a consensual democracy was to convince thousands of conservative agrarians to remain inactive, and for the greater good watch the ravaging of their farms from the safety of Athenian ramparts. Ironically, the sheer size of the Spartan-led invasion – sources variously claim it to have been 30,000 to 60,000 strong – made the Peloponnesians' hoped-for encounter with the Athenian army of considerably less than 20,000 hoplites highly unlikely.

Athens, once besieged, increasingly imported food and material into her port at Piraeus, while still sending her magnificent fleet to stabilize her maritime empire and to prevent Peloponnesian infiltrations. Local cavalry

*On this rare black-figure vase of the sixth century two early Greek open galleys –
often known as aphracts – are pictured with light hulls, a symbolic rower on a single
deck, small rams, and large sails. The tendency in Hellenistic times for gigantism – the
building of massive unwieldy ships – made states realize the importance of having a
number of small, more mobile ships.*

patrols helped to keep the devastation of Attica to a minimum. From 430
to 421 Athenian ships were constantly active in the Aegean, western
Greece, north at the Chalcidice, and off the coast of the Peloponnese,
keeping allies loyal and landing troops where they were needed to
neutralize Spartan inroads. Under this proactive strategy of attrition,
Athens did not need to defeat the Spartan army or its allied Peloponnesian
fleet. Rather, it sought both to keep the blinkered Spartans busy protecting
their allies from sudden enemy depredations and to warn all neutral states
that Athenian ships were right over the horizon, and could arrive far more
quickly in any crisis than hoplites marching up from Laconia.

   This Periclean strategy of passive defense inside Attica and attrition
abroad ostensibly made sense. But it ignored two critical considerations:
first, the psychological toll on the evacuated citizenry of Attica and the

horrendous conditions inside the city, which quickly led to the great plague of 430–428 that eventually left a quarter of her population dead and as many others indignant and miserable refugees; second, the reliance on the personal magnetism of Pericles himself to rein in the expansionist and often foolhardy dreams of the Athenian *dêmos*. His death of the plague in 429 at the outset of the war ensured that his policy of containment and exhaustion would be modified and eventually dropped for more aggressive enterprises. Pericles' plan never to lose a war had little appeal to demagogues and rhetoricians who could envision each Athenian triumph not as a key to successful stalemate of the Spartan phalanx, but as part of a more ambitious plan of total conquest.

And two events in the Archidamian war quickly proved more conclusive than did sitting behind the walls of Athens or raiding the seaboard of the Peloponnese. In a brilliant strategic move, the Athenian demagogue Cleon led an expeditionary force to occupy Pylos and the nearby island of Sphacteria off the western coast of Messenia (425). This unexpected toehold in the western Peloponnese cut off a number of Spartan hoplites – 292 were taken prisoner – and ensured that scores of helots could flock to the Athenian sanctuary. In one bold stroke, Athens had hit at the two worst fears in the Spartan psyche: apprehension over helot rebellion and paranoia over the capture and humiliation of her purportedly invincible hoplites. Indeed, Athens threatened to kill all the captives if a Spartan army set foot in Attica – and after 425 they did not. The Pylos campaign revealed the entire frailty of the Spartan system of helotage; without its serfs, the professional army of Spartiates would have to farm and thus might become little more than a feared local constabulary. Other city states took note for the future.

The other alternative to passive defence lay in pitched hoplite battle; and in 424 the Athenians unfortunately learned just how unwise it was to face an army of the caliber of the Thebans. To end their two-front dilemma, the Athenian generals Demosthenes and Hippocrates intended to attack Boeotia from the north and south, by land and sea. That overly ambitious plan failed – long-distance communications in ancient war were always nearly impossible – and the army under Hippocrates was left facing superior Theban infantry alone near the small sanctuary at Delium near the Athenian–Boeotian border in a battle emblematic of the entire evolution in hoplite tactics and values. No longer were hoplite battles one-dimensional collisions of lumbering armoured men.

The enemy Theban general Pagondas was both aggressive and something of a tactician, stacking his hoplites twenty-five shields deep on his right wing. Despite the uphill run – terrain would now be a consideration in hoplite battle – the Athenian right wing under their general Hippocrates (who, in the tradition of defeated Greek generals, would not survive the battle) quickly cut down the Boeotian confederates opposite. These victorious Athenians on the right then made a complete circle, so much so that the two companies of their pincers crashed together, 'fell into chaos, mistook, and so killed each other'.

The enemy Boeotians inside the ring were annihilated. These were brave but greenhorn farmers from the villages around Thebes. The male population of the small Boeotian city state of Thespiae was almost entirely wiped out by the Athenian charge – a bitter irony for the Thespians, since many of their ancestors had died bravely for the Greek cause alongside the Spartans at Thermopylae, had had their city destroyed by the Persians, had regrouped at Plataea the next year, had their walls dismantled by their suspicious Theban allies the year after Delium (423) and would perish almost to a man once more at the battle of Coronea (394) against the Peloponnesians, thirty years hence. The history of Classical Thespiae is the century-long story of the butchery of her citizens in arms.

Meanwhile across the battlefield the Theban general Pagondas 'gradually at first' pushed the Athenians left downhill, and was systematically clearing the battlefield through the advantage of favourable terrain and superior weight of his deep mass. Only when the slaughter of his own allies threatened to pour Athenian hoplites to his rear did he devise something unheard of in the history of Greek warfare. Still maintaining the pressure on the right, he dispatched a *reserve* of cavalry to the left around the rear of the hill to stave off the Athenians.

To the successful but exhausted Athenians under Hippocrates the idea that cavalry would play a decisive role in phalanx battle was startling, even more so the notion that such fresh troops on the horizon were still uncommitted and appearing out of nowhere behind the hill. Busy spearing Boeotians, yanked apart with difficulty from killing each other, flush with the revelation the battle was won, the Athenians suddenly imagined an entirely new army, and thus no rest for their labors, however previously successful. They now went from blood-drunk frenzy to profound depression.

At this juncture, Pagondas took his cue, pressed on, and knocked apart the Athenian line before him. Soon the entire Athenian army was 'in panic' – the once victorious and savage right wing now non-existent, the left wearied, beaten down and fragmented by the pressure of the accumulated shields of Pagondas' phalanx.

This dusk run home from Delium to Attica became a veritable who's who of famous Athenians. Anecdotes abound about the particular conduct of notables in the disastrous, confused, night-time escape from marauding enemy horse and skirmishers, enemies who now ventured on unchecked into Attica. Pursuit after hoplite battle was no longer to be discouraged. Plato tells us in his *Symposium* that Socrates, although forty-five, 'strutted like a proud marsh-goose', backpedaling with a small group of determined infantry, and thereby forcing any opportunistic pursuer to go on to easier game. In that sense he becomes enshrined as the paragon of middling hoplite virtue, and it is impossible to envision the founder of western philosophy as either a mounted grandee or a crafty archer – or dead twenty-five years before his famous trial. In another Platonic

Plato

dialogue, Laches, perhaps nearer to fifty, adds that he accompanied Socrates, and felt that had other Athenians emulated the philosopher's infantry resolve, the army would have been saved (over 1,000 Athenians died, most of them in the panicked stampede). We hear, too, that the 26-year-old Alcibiades rode through the disintegrated ranks looking to aid hoplites like Socrates, who were besieged by light-armed troops. Plato's stepfather, Pyrilampes, nearly 55 years old in 424, was wounded by a javelin and then captured when he fled to Mount Parnes.

Military historians have noted the ambitious strategic plans of the Athenians, and are impressed by the Thebans' tactical innovations at Delium, which in themselves marked a new departure in hoplite battle: terrain, reserves, increased depth of shields and horsemen were now as important as the nerve and muscular strength of agrarian infantry. Much of the later battle plan of the Theban general Epaminondas – deep columns, close concert of cavalry and infantry – was evident fifty years earlier here. But in the collective memory of the Athenians, Delium simply remained a black day, when hundreds of her most notable had been speared and cut down in a desperate night-time run home. And the ripples of Delium were felt in Athens – and in the West in general – for centuries. Had Alcibiades been killed or disgraced at Delium, the Athenians would never have gone to Sicily nine years later, and thus would probably not have lost the Peloponnesian war. Had Socrates been a little less adroit, and fallen in the retreat, the course of western philosophy would have been radically altered. Euripides' magnificent tragedy, the *Suppliants*, produced the next year at Athens, was prompted by the disgraceful Theban treatment of the Athenian dead at Delium. And at Thebes the municipal center underwent an artistic and architectural renaissance from the spoils and sale of booty gathered from the killed and retreating Athenians.

Yet strategically the Theban victory at Delium did little for Spartan war aims. Her helots were still deserting and she ceased sending into Attica hoplites who could neither draw out the Athenian army nor reduce the city economically. The idea had once been that all Greek farmers would fight if they saw a few acres of their grain torched, some vines trampled, or olive-trees cut. Agricultural devastation was the traditional trigger in Greek warfare to instigate the pitched battle at which the Spartans so excelled. For nearly three centuries the idea for every Greek army had been to march into the enemy plain, synchronizing the onslaught with the May ripening of wheat and barley. If everything went right, the invaders might arrive right before the crop was to be harvested, forcing farmers in this bizarre brand of agricultural poker either to fight to protect their year's work or to watch their city's food supply go up in flames in a matter of minutes.

But in the past, devastation had been a catalyst for war, not a comprehensive strategy to starve out an enemy, especially an adversary as flexible and resilient as Athens. And the problem was not merely that Athens could be supplied by sea from Piraeus or that Athenian cavalry patrols hampered ravaging parties. There were intrinsic problems in the previously untried tactic of systematically destroying the agricultural infrastructure of an entire countryside. The Spartans quickly learned that it was difficult to reach the grainfields at their precise moment of vulnerability. Too early an entry and the grain was still green and not combustible, requiring the time-consuming and largely inefficient process of trampling and cutting widely scattered parcels. If they came too late, the defenders might work overtime and get the crop inside the walls, leaving the enemy only stubble from which to search out a few provisions. And agrarian hoplites from the Peloponnese had their own crops to harvest precisely at the time that they were miles away in Attica. Enemy horsemen, who were ineffective against hoplites in formation, became formidable opponents when riding down infantry, plundering and ravaging in pockets of twos and threes.

True, we hear of Spartan attacks on Attic houses, orchards and vineyards. But here too timing was critical. It was best to arrive right at the grape or olive harvest – as the Spartans did at Acanthus in northern Greece in 424 – where occupation might circumvent picking and so entail the loss of the entire crop, requiring capitulation of an entire *polis* dependent on viticulture. Vineyards and orchards could be cut, and occasionally torched if enough dry fuel was near, but that required enormous effort and even then only weakened but did not kill the tree or vine. Again, it was usually a question of losing the annual harvest, not the destruction of generations of agricultural investment. Houses, as in the Boeotian raiding in Attica in the latter part of the Peloponnesian war, were plundered and knocked down. But most often the valuable woodwork was already evacuated, leaving the walls of mud-brick and the roof tiles that were not combustible and easily replaceable through manufacture of native clays. In short, for a decade's worth of war against the Athenians the Spartans had accomplished very little in Attica. What losses the Athenians had incurred – and they were considerable – were due to the unforeseen consequences of the plague of 430–428 and the infantry fatalities at Delium.

Agricultural devastation was a strategic option in all the great invasions of Greek history, where warfare transcended the old notion of a single hoplite battle and entered the realm of economic warfare – the Persian inroads of 480–79, the Spartan attacks during the Archidamian war of 431–421, the occupation of Attica during the Decelean war of 413–404, and Epaminondas' four marches into the Peloponnese from 371 to 362. Yet even in these cases, while crop losses are noted and the predominantly agrarian nature of ancient societies is unquestioned, agricultural damage played little role in the eventual outcome of the war. To win, the Persians knew that they had to destroy the Greek navy and army at Salamis and Plataea, rather than try to starve the city states by attacking the agriculture of Greece. During the Peloponnesian war King Archidamus first sought to meet hoplites on open ground, not to wreck abandoned farms. The Spartan fort at Decelea was valuable – but not decisive in itself to the later Spartan success – because of enormous plunder, slave desertions, political intrigue, and prevention of access to Attica. The Thebans destroyed Spartan hegemony through the sponsorship of fortified states like Messene, Megalopolis and Mantinea, not by starving the Spartans through the devastation of vines, grain and trees.

When the Spartan firebrand Brasidas and his Athenian counterpart Cleon – the comic playwright Aristophanes' mortar and pestle of this infernal war – were killed in a proxy engagement to the north near Amphipolis, both sides realized the futility of the conflict, and the so-called Archidamian war (431–421) ended in stalemate. The Athenians surrendered all the Spartan prisoners they had taken on Sphacteria and dismantled their base there, removing somewhat the specter of helot insurrection. Sparta and Thebes, in turn, ceased their invasions of Attica and all parties agreed to maintain the situation as it was before the war. Neither side gained much strategic advantage for the ten years of killing and destruction. The cost to Athens of manning the fleet and conducting sieges and raids was enormous; for the same expense of running the war, the city could have built *two* new Parthenons *every year*. Victory in the future would require more imaginative strategy, greater manpower, and additional sources of financial capital. Pragmatists at both Athens and Sparta, restless for more war, now looked for the first time to the gold of Persia.

In the later surrogate wars during the so-called peace of Nicias between 421 and 415, ironically Athens used her hoplites in combined maritime operations, whereas Sparta and her allies in time developed a competent fleet: during the entire course of the Peloponnesian war there were not more than three or four hoplite battles of the old style. And even these engagements at Delium, Solygeia, Mantinea and Syracuse had no role in bringing the war itself to a decisive conclusion. Both belligerents now turned to a variety of secondary theaters throughout the Aegean world and Asia Minor, stirring up allies and investigating new alliances until hostilities formally resumed. Persia conspired to check Athenian imperialism and win back Ionia by subsidizing the creation of a Spartan fleet – an armada of 500 Peloponnesian ships was envisioned – prompting Athens to renew her efforts to arouse the Peloponnese. In 418 the brilliant but reckless Athenian general Alcibiades engineered a grand alliance of Peloponnesian states to challenge Spartan hegemony at Mantinea. Despite the bravery of the Argives and Mantineans, Sparta crushed the insurgency with its feared charge on the right by its crack Spartiate élite. The Peloponnese was secure; oligarchs at Argos now turned the city toward the Spartan cause, and the Athenians gave up all further direct confrontation with Spartan infantry. The independent-minded states of the Peloponnese would have to wait half a century for the arrival of Epaminondas and his Theban farmers.

Athenian strategists sought more indirect aggression elsewhere. Ostensibly Sicily seemed a logical prize; its large navy challenged Athenian maritime supremacy, and its mercenaries and transport ships had on occasion lent aid to the Peloponnesians. Moreover, to the Athenian Assembly, the conquest of Syracuse, Sicily's largest city, promised rich booty and additional imperial revenues. Some even talked of Sicily as the launching pad for future aggrandizement against Carthage. The frenzied voices of the Assembly – led on by Alcibiades of Delium fame – cared little that Syracuse was over 800 miles distant, had abundant financial reserves, good cavalry and a superb fleet, much less that it was a democratic state – or that undefeated Spartan and Theban infantry remained nearby on both home fronts, and a growing

The departure for war was a favourite scene of classical vase painters, who usually idealized and personalized the farewell in the manner of Homeric epic. The warriors are usually young virile hoplites, with impressive armour, and clear signs of wealth such as the chariot here depicted. In reality, most families gathered together their male members – in cases of dire emergency all those ranging in age from 21 to 62 – brought along the slaves, packed up three days rations and their panoplies, and then trekked into the agora of the nearby community, where they were joined by other rural farmers.

Peloponnesian fleet was now sailing in the Athenian waters of the Aegean. Thucydides provides an ambivalent assessment of the enterprise (415–413), emphasizing the foolhardy ambition so typical of imperial democracy, and yet, as a military man, obviously impressed with the sheer scale of operations. He faults lack of support at home for the venture, but in fact the Athenians emptied their city, sending additional good men and *matériel* to be lost in what was a bad idea from the start.

In two successive and enormous armadas, 40,000–60,000 Athenians and their allies – a megalomaniac idea of an entire empire in arms – fought for more than two years against the only other large democracy in the Greek world. With help from the new Peloponnesian fleet, the Syracusans co-ordinated the Sicilian defence, destroyed all the Athenian ships, captured or killed the entire invading army, and executed the Athenian generals. It was the costliest expedition in the history of Classical Greek warfare, consuming over 20 million drachmas – enough to build *all* the monuments and temples on the Athenian acropolis and then some.

Almost 40,000 of those who sailed were either dead or enslaved – a casualty rate forty times higher than the Athenian hoplite disaster at Delium. Thucydides summarizes the Athenian débâcle as outright military extermination. 'The Athenians,' he says of their catastrophe on Sicily, 'were beaten at all areas and altogether; all that they suffered was great; they were annihilated, as the saying goes, with a total annihilation, their fleet, their army – everything was annihilated, and few out of many returned home.'

Sparta immediately systematically garrisoned Decelea, 15 miles from Athens herself, to encourage desertions from rural Attica and local disruptions in commerce, all the while applying steady pressure to pry away tribute-paying Athenian allies in the Aegean, the life-blood of the city's capital and military reserves. Now the Spartans were in Attica year-round, and wisely more interested in plunder, slave desertion and political insurrection than in chopping down trees in the vain hope of an Athenian infantry response. For economic warfare to be effective in the ancient world, hostile troops needed to be present on a daily basis, preventing farmers from reaching their crops, offering sanctuary to runaway slaves, and providing a clearing house for stolen property, as well as a support base for traitors and insurrectionists. In that sense, the Spartans did more economic damage in the initial year of their occupation at Decelea (415) than during all the seasonal invasions of the Archidamian war (431–425). And while the Athenian fleet held out for another decade against the combined Peloponnesian armada, and the army and cavalry kept the enemy infantry from the city proper, the end was never in doubt after Sicily and Decelea. After two oligarchic coups in 411 and 404 inside the city, and the loss of the entire fleet at Aegospotami (404), Athens was exhausted, morally, spiritually and materially.

The Peloponnesian war was not merely an example of the destructiveness and brutality of western warfare when divorced from cultural restraint, but, as Thucydides noted, 'a harsh teacher' of the human condition itself. The three-century tradition of a free Greek citizenry to question authority and to re-examine the logic of war was renewed as never before, ensuring that this novel war was now looked upon mostly unfavourably in all genres of Classical literature, from drama to history to philosophy. Remember, too, that in nearly all city states, generals and commanders were elected officials and under constant civilian audit subject to the whim of public opinion. All notable Greek generals – Pausanias, Miltiades, Themistocles, Aristides, Cimon, Pericles, Alcibiades, Lysander and Epaminondas – were either exiled, sacked, indicted or fined at some point in their careers. The eight Athenian generals responsible for the *victory* at the sea-battle at Arginusae (406) were executed by the democracy for failing to rescue survivors from their own disabled triremes. Criticism of war and the conduct of fighting were not parlour games in the ancient city state.

Greek literature had always reflected civic scrutiny of this kind. Often there is a general lament for the terrible cost of fighting and a repugnance for organized bloodletting. So Homer's Zeus tell Ares, the war god, 'To me you are the most hateful of all gods who hold Olympus. Forever quarreling is dear to your heart, wars and battles.' The aged Nestor later on in the *Iliad* said nearly the same thing about fighting between Greeks: 'Out of all brotherhood, outlawed, homeless, shall be the man who longs for all the horror of fighting among his own people.' Odd sentiments in a poem which was purportedly honouring martial gallantry. The Greeks believed that war was innate to the human species and a part of civilized culture itself; but that pessimism did not imply that they felt particular wars were always wise, humane, or necessary.

Archilochus of Paros, the seventh-century poet, was more lighthearted in his distaste for battle to the death: 'Some barbarian is waving my shield, since I was forced to leave that perfectly fine piece of equipment under a bush. But I escaped, so what does it matter? Let the shield go. I can buy another one just as good.' Many hoplites surely agreed. The poet Sappho objected to the predominant male view that put too much emphasis on military life: the fairest sight was not horsemen, infantry or ships – but 'I say she whom one loves best is the loveliest'. Pindar, the early fifth-century Theban poet, saw no glory in killing. Ever the realist, he warned that war 'was a sweet thing to him who does not know it, but to him who has made trial of it, it is a thing of fear'. To Herodotus, whose history is an encomium of the Greeks' defence of their homeland, war was a perverse travesty, when fathers buried sons rather than vice versa. Sophocles, an admiral at the brutal siege of Samos in 440, has the chorus in his tragedy, *Ajax*, cry, 'Whoever it was that first revealed to Greece ubiquitous war with its hateful arms, I curse him! Would that the sky or the impartial house of Hades had taken him first. Generations of suffering upon suffering he wrought, for he was a destroyer of men.' At its genesis, western warfare faced sharp criticism, constant audit, and public efforts to end it.

But as the Peloponnesian war dragged on, in Athens the traditional complaints reached new levels of passion and anger against a futile policy of attrition that brought no clear-cut victory for either side. Thucydides records with empathy the bitterness of the citizens of rural Attica who wished to return home to their farms and cease hostilities with the Spartan invaders, and gives a deliberately graphic description of the annihilation of the small Greek communities of Mycalessus and Melos. Similarly, Aristophanes' comedies *Acharnians*, *Peace* and *Lysistrata* all centre around commonplace farmers or neglected women who alone have enough sense to see that the fighting of the Peloponnesian war must end immediately in any way possible. In these plays 'Treaties', 'Peace' and 'Reconciliation' are near-divine entities, which bring in their wake food, drink, sexuality, singing, dancing – and despair to sour and rapacious magistrates, politicians and arms-sellers, who are mocked and ridiculed before the audience by name.

Euripides' *Trojan Women* was produced in 415, right after the Athenian slaughter of the Melians, on the eve of the great expedition to Sicily and its eventual catastrophe. The dramatist makes Cassandra condemn the Greek invasion to Troy on a variety of moral grounds; her caustic indictment makes little effort to hide Euripides' own obvious disgust with Athenian depravity in its ongoing conflict against Sparta and her allies.

Fourth-century philosophers continued to complain of the radical transformations in Greek warfare accelerated by the Peloponnesian war. Plato's Socrates objects to the continual devastation of Greek land and property, and to the stripping of corpses, while Xenophon, veteran of a Panhellenic mercenary expedition to Asia, explored alternatives to hostilities in his philosophical works. Both he and Aristotle were concerned about the financial costs incurred by lengthy sieges and maritime campaigns. And by the mid fourth century, Athenian orators like Isocrates denounced war altogether in Greece. In various speeches he called for a 'Common Peace', in which exhaustive killing would cease, allowing bankrupt state treasuries to recover and prosperity to return. Far better it was to punish the Persian who had financed many of the forces in the Peloponnesian war than to kill fellow Greeks – Plato had earlier remarked that Greeks and barbarians 'were natural enemies', not squabbling cousins.

By the time the Peloponnesian war had ended, its initial belligerents had radically changed – the Spartans were now a naval power, the Athenians masters of sea-borne infantry operations. The inaugural leadership – Archidamus in Sparta, Pericles in Athens – along with thousands of early zealots were long dead; and the original causes of the conflict largely forgotten by those who pressed on with the fight. This endless cycle of challenge–response–counter-response took on a twenty-seven-year life of its own and ruined the old Hellenic idea that war served the *polis*, rather than the *polis* war. In short, the Peloponnesian war was a broad canvas, in which the best and worst of western culture were fleshed in with broad strokes all at once: the Greeks' frightening ingenuity at finding ever more ways to kill soldiers and civilians, and at the same time their perplexing tendency to employ the freedom, courage and brilliance of their best minds to deplore just such abject stupidity.

AN ARMY TO REMEMBER

What were the military lessons to be learnt from the Peloponnesian war? That it cost money. A single year of Athenian-style war by land and sea would bankrupt the majority of the Greek city states. Temples such as those to Apollo at Bassae, Aphaea on Aegina, or Apollo at Delphi required intricate financing and took years to construct; yet the Athenians alone could have built all three in a single year with what they spent each season during the Peloponnesian war. Aristophanes complained bitterly of the Athenian welfare state that paid the disabled, unemployed, poor and aged (a mob of some 5,000 to 10,000?) to serve on juries, attend the theatre, or become government clerks. But for the price of the Sicilian expedition, it would have been far cheaper for Athens to have hired its entire citizen population of 40,000 at full wages to sit and do nothing for a year – and kept them safe in the bargain.

On the purely tactical level, shock battle was proven to be still a dramatic way to obliterate the infantry of an opponent, as both the fights at Delium (424) and Mantinea (418) had shown. Such dramatic and horrific engagements employed in a wider strategic context would

In this early black-figure vase a solitary hoplite demonstrates through his footwork, spear-thrusting and shield-handling that there was more skill to the fighting than mere pushing.

remain the hallmark of western warfare well after the death of Alexander. Hoplite helmets and body protection were now lighter, and rudimentary manoeuvre – mostly the manipulation of terrain and crude attempts at envelopment and the use of reserve forces – sometimes made pitched battle more than the simple collisions of heavy infantry. Still, there were few states who were any longer ready to entrust their entire defense to heavy infantry. The victory of Sparta meant that any hoplite fighting by necessity entailed meeting the dreaded Spartan phalanx in open battle – in fact, every major hoplite conflict of the fourth century until Chaeronea raised the unpleasant spectre of charging into the line of Spartan red-cloaks.

Yet, if hoplites could win pitched battles, material resources and preparedness won wars – and the two were no longer the same thing. Once the connection between citizenship and military service was destroyed, many Greek armies preferred to augment infantry with more flexible light-armed troops and missile-throwers. Cultural and social concerns were secondary to killing the enemy as efficiently as possible. The ability of Athens to withstand from their walls the Spartan invasions of the Archidamian war, and in turn the invulnerability of the Spartan fort at Decelea, proved that, in an age before heavy artillery, fortified positions were nearly invulnerable from attack, and as bases for combined operations might be used for more than simple passive defence. In turn, the way to assault an enemy inside fortifications was not with hoplites climbing the ramparts on ladders or cutting down trees in the plain, but by designing an entire new generation of siege engines, whose intricacy and mobility – at exorbitant cost – aimed to knock down ever longer, taller – and more expensive – walls.

Moreover, throughout the Peloponnesian war, the poor and slaves, as well as mercenaries, had been used by both sides. The Spartan general Brasidas in northern Greece had used 1,700 hoplites who were freed helots, and the crews of Athenian triremes were exclusively manned by the landless. In the latter years of the war, all triremes were increasingly augmented with slaves, perhaps reaching ratios in which over half the rowers were servile. By the 390s there were more freed helots in the Spartan army than Spartiate Similars. Sheer military necessity, not abstractions like agrarianism or citizenship, now dictated how and when a city state fought, ensuring a far more innovative military, but also undermining the entire idea that the *polis* was to be defended cheaply by a community of yeoman citizen farmers.

The Greek states had no solutions for the new paradoxes of the Peloponnesian war. Hired troops, the growing science of logistics, and the technology of siegecraft and fortification cost far more than a column of hoplites – and meant taxes, the old anathema to the agrarian city state. But those eligible for public infantry service were now an increasing minority of the resident population and not eager to fight beyond the border without money – and the muster of hoplites in itself could no longer ensure the safety of the city state anyway.

A brutal cycle was now established: income, property and excise taxes would be raised to pay for military expenditures. This in turn further weakened the agrarian fabric of the *polis*, which meant even fewer yeoman hoplites for military service. Armies then grew still more mercenary – requiring yet more money from a dwindling pool of hard-working farmers. Farmers left the countryside for the army, since they preferred to receive wages than pay taxes – a cycle which was also to be repeated in the last two centuries of the Roman republic when warfare beyond local borders similarly evolved to serve less than egalitarian interests. Because of this dramatic revolution in warfare, Greek society throughout the fourth century gradually moved to a culture of two, not three, classes: the few who owned the land and the many who worked it and protected it for others.

Recent archaeological surveys of the Greek countryside confirm a gradual diminution in rural habitation toward the end of the fourth century – a trend not begun by the losses in themselves of farms during the Peloponnesian war, but rather by more subtle and insidious practices inaugurated during that conflict. In essence, Greek history was operating in reverse: fourth-century warfare was increasingly fought for plunder and autocracy, waged by élites followed by the poor and mercenary – precisely the Dark Age conditions of centuries past that the city state and its hoplite agenda had once superseded. No wonder, then, that massive Hellenistic tombs for the war dead were rarely publicly inspired or communal, but enormously costly and gaudy private temples and altars for a few autocrats – all a return to the ideology of the shaft grave, chamber tomb and tholos of the pre-*polis*.

On the strategic level, the increasing ferocity of the Peloponnesian war honed the skills of Greek armies and navies to a degree unmatched elsewhere in the Mediterranean. Indeed, Persian intervention in the war was limited to transfers of capital, not direct military support, which probably would have been of little use. Far more Greeks died in the Peloponnesian war than were killed by Persians in all the battles on land and sea, from Marathon in 490 to Alexander's final triumph at Gaugamela in 331. The Peloponnesian war established a general truth that would last well into modern times: the real danger for any western army was always another western army.

The complexity of the new Hellenic way of war and the vulnerability of non-Greeks to its application were also illustrated as soon as hostilities ceased. In 401 the claimant to the Persian throne, Cyrus the Younger, enlisted nearly 10,000 Greek mercenaries – mostly skilled unemployed veterans from Arcadia and Achaea in the Peloponnese – to ensure his dynastic succession. Xenophon's remarkable eyewitness account, the *Anabasis* ('The March up Country'), chronicles their 1,500-mile trek to Babylon, the subsequent hoplite prowess at the losing battle of Cunaxa (401) – Cyrus threw away the Greeks' victory by a rash fatal charge against his hated brother Artaxerxes – and the heroic 2,000-mile return march through Media, Carduchia, Armenia, back to the safety of Byzantium.

The eye-opening success of the Ten Thousand in marching right through Persian territory brought home a number of truths to Greek military thinkers: first, Greek soldiers could live off the rich land of Persia, and in times of duress quite systematically – and democratically – organize sophisticated foraging and supply parties that could sustain thousands for months in the field; second, the battle at Cunaxa and its aftermath proved that no infantry in the world could withstand a hoplite phalanx that was protected on its flanks; and third, Greece possessed skilled light-armed troops and horsemen, who, with proper training and integration with heavy infantry, might enhance and protect hoplites marching in difficult terrain and against a variety of enemy archers, cavalry and irregulars. The success of the Ten Thousand underscored that, without the ethical bridle of agrarianism, Greek military practice could now be a partner to the general Hellenic economic and scientific dynamism that had already been pre-eminent in the Mediterranean for nearly a century.

Within three years the Spartans were in Persian territory ostensibly to ensure the freedom of the Ionian Greeks. In fact, aided by the remnants of the Ten Thousand, their integrated hoplite and mounted forces began plundering the satrapies of the Great King along the eastern shore of the Aegean in preparation for an expected showdown with Artaxerxes' grand army. By 396, under the command of the Spartan king Agesilaus, the Peloponnesians were planning further large attacks against the interior of Persia herself. However, Persia had soon financed a new Athenian fleet that won a resounding victory over the Peloponnesian ships off Cnidus in August 394 in south-western Asia Minor. In addition, Persian gold had helped to organize an anti-Spartan Hellenic coalition back in Greece, which threatened to invade the Peloponnese in the absence of Agesilaus' main force fighting overseas.

Agesilaus was forced to withdraw his Spartan hoplites to meet the Greek armies on the mainland, freeing Persia from the spectre of Greek invasion for the next half century. At the Nemea river near Corinth (394), the home Spartan army and its Peloponnesian allies defeated a coalition of Argives, Corinthians, Thebans and Athenians in the greatest hoplite battle since Plataea. And weeks later Agesilaus himself on his return from Asia Minor repeated the outcome of Nemea; his returning veteran expeditionaries met the Thebans at Coronea in Boeotia in a head-to-head charge that pitted experienced professionals against tough rustics – 'a battle like none other of our time', the historian and probable eye-witness Xenophon remarked. By 387 Persia, Thebes, Athens and Sparta made peace, and the so-called Corinthian war ended. The inability of the Spartans to manage the old Athenian overseas hegemony of the Greeks was made clear; yet her mastery of the conservative tenets of hoplite battle for a while longer kept her oligarchic alliance in the Peloponnese intact.

True, Sparta had won the Peloponnesian war and for the next quarter century had proven unbeatable in hoplite battle. But its police state proved the least capable of the major city states of inheriting either the

Athenian hegemony or the spiritual leadership of Greece. Her economy was not monetary and her hoplite population was small and declining – and war was now demanding money and numbers, not just nerve and muscle. Control of the increasingly restless helots meant that expeditions ideally must be short. And for Spartan commanders and hoplites to retain the harsh discipline of their military indoctrination, they could not be on duty for long periods away from their wall-less, money-less and entertainment-less *polis*. Yet, on average, in the decades following the Peloponnesian war twenty or more of their best generals were now stationed away from Sparta every year, some for as long as five to ten years in succession. Exposure to overseas gold, luxuries and commerce could only undermine their commanders' adherence to Laconism – the corruption of Spartan notables like Lysander was, in fact, a popular topos in Greek literature of the fourth century.

Yet the greatest weakness in the entire military system of Sparta remained the simple absence of manpower. Aristotle remarks that by the later fourth century there were not more than 1,500 full Spartiate citizens, though the countryside of Laconia might have supported 30,000 – every other class in Laconia and Messenia multiplied except the Similars, who were on patrol or in the barracks in their twenties, when they might instead have married and raised families.

In the chaotic world of fourth-century Greece campaigning could last for months, and the ubiquity of new technology and mercenaries sapped human and financial resources at astronomical rates. Sparta, however, sought to retain its rigid barracks life, in which all males over the age of seven joined group messes as the age of marriage continued to be delayed by mandatory drill and campaigning. Constant fighting in the sixty years following the outbreak of the Peloponnesian war had reduced the reservoir of military-age males by the sheer wear and tear of their continual service abroad. Even her infantry forces by the fourth century were overwhelmingly allied or filled out by Laconians of inferior status. Perhaps the ratio of Spartiates to others in the phalanx was approaching one to five, and worse yet, most of these scarce Similars were stationed in the most vulnerable positions on the line where casualties were most likely, either around the king or as file-leaders and front-line hoplites.

Clearly, then, military supremacy under the new rules of Greek warfare meant manpower and capital, which explains why by 377 the irrepressible Athenian maritime democracy was once again resurgent and in control of a second though less imperialistic sea-league. Yet, the real power in Greece for nearly a decade (371–362) was across the Attic border at Thebes. Its sudden prominence demands explanation. The Theban military operated in something of a paradox: a reactionary reliance on hoplites, and yet subtle refinements in the tactics and strategy of phalanx warfare that might lend the old arm a deadly new destructiveness if used under careful strategic considerations of time and space.

First, it is crucial to remember that Boeotia consisted of a series of enormously large and fertile plains. By the 370s its numerous autonomous city states were federated, and thus for the first time in Greek history the entire region marshalled its material and human resource into a natural and truly unified democratic entity. The Boeotians were under nominal Theban leadership, their agricultural area was richer and more extensive than Attica, and their population, at nearly 100,000, was larger than Laconia – and they saw no reason to tolerate political subservience to either.

Moreover, Theban diehard faith in hoplites had a certain logic. Navies, fortifications, siegecraft, mercenaries and missile troops were expensive and largely necessary for campaigning outside the protective plains of mainland Greece. Yet, if a state's strategic vision was largely defensive – fighting in and around its own inland territory – or at least confined to a few days' march from its home, traditional hoplite armies still remained invincible and extremely cheap. Even if other city states did not play by the old rules, all potential invaders would eventually have to cross the plain of Boeotia and thereupon meet the Theban phalanx on flat ground. In an accessible flatland like Boeotia – the great battles of Greek history from Plataea to Chaeronea were all fought there – infantry in mass still made sense.

The trick now was to protect the old phalanx tactically from new challenges of combined forces and to ensure that the old civic faith in public military service remained strong. The Thebans under the leadership of the elected generals, Epaminondas and Pelopidas,

The shield explains much of the nature of hoplite warfare. Its great size and weight required the full employment of the left arm, The arm-ring (porpax) and hand-grip (antilabê) here shown allowed the 20-pound shield to be held chest-high with the single arm. Modern simulations suggest few men can hold 20-pound shields out from the body for more than a few minutes.

accomplished both brilliantly. First, Boeotia remained largely agrarian. Without a large number of ships – a small fleet of twelve triremes was expanded, but largely abandoned after a couple of years – fortifications and mercenaries, taxes remained largely non-existent. The federated system of representative and constitutional government curtailed infighting, and thus most surrounding agrarian communities willingly contributed their farmer hoplites to the Boeotian cause.

Second, tactical innovations sought to enhance the inherent strengths of Boeotian infantry, which in antiquity had a reputation for muscular strength and combative ferocity. From the battle of Delium (424) onward, Thebans had massed more deeply than the hoplite standard of eight shields, their columns ranging from sixteen to twenty-five, and at Leuctra fifty men deep. True, the flanks of such a massed phalanx were more exposed by the deeper column. And the initial killing power of offensive weaponry was reduced as more spearmen were taken out of the first three ranks (who alone could reach the enemy in the inaugural onslaught) and stacked to the rear. But in turn, the Thebans gained enormous penetrating power, as accumulated shields created greater thrust – the ideal was that the sheer physicality of Boeotian yeomen might punch a hole and then push right through the enemy before they were overwhelmed on the flanks. In Classical tactical parlance, Epaminondas has refined the tradition of applying equal pressure along the battle line into a concentration of force on the left wing, realizing that in past battles, victory was achieved on the horns anyway.

A deeper phalanx also reinforced the notion of revolutionary *élan*, and in our sources there is a definite sense that the Thebans in mass often broke through enemy ranks because they thought they could. Unlike the more skilled Spartans who walked to the music of flutes, and whose drilling might allow complicated reversals of direction and flanking movements, the amateurishness of Boeotian farmers found a natural outlet in sheer brute strength and the rolling momentum of mass attack. The best veterans of the lot would both man the blade of the phalanx and hold the rear tight, while those strong but less experienced might push from the middle.

The general Epaminondas added a couple of vital ancillary tactical touches. The Theban mass and fighting élite would be placed on the left of the Boeotian battle line, *not* the right, in order to smash the opposite élite royal right of the Spartan phalanx – the history of Boeotian pitched battle in the first half of the fourth century is mostly a story of fighting Spartans – destroying the morale of the entire Peloponnesian army, and pre-empting the known Spartan tendency to roll up the enemy by initiating a flanking movement from its right. In addition, specialized contingents on the right – the famous 'Sacred Band' of 150 erotic partners is the best known – and the use of integrated cavalry tactics ensured that native Boeotians themselves could protect their new ponderous and unwieldy columns from enemy light-armed skirmishers and peltasts. Tradition had it that Pelopidas led the Sacred Band at the 'cutting edge' of the battle line – apparently these crack and rather fanatical troops would be the wedge that prepared the way for the mass behind. Specialized *hamippoi*, or light-armed troops trained to fight alongside cavalry, protected the flanks and added flexibility to the charge of horsemen.

The result was the creation of the most deadly infantry in the history of Classical Greek warfare. At Leuctra in 371 the Theban phalanx led its outnumbered Boeotian allies right through the Spartans, killing King Cleombrotus himself, annihilating 400 of the élite and increasingly scarce Spartiates, and hundreds more of their Laconian and Peloponnesian allies. Nearly every one of the Similars on the Spartan right wing that faced the Theban steamroller – eighty shields in breadth, fifty in depth – perished. Since Sparta had remained unwalled, and its defence predicated entirely on the martial courage of just those hoplites, in theory there was nothing now to prevent the Theban onslaught into the streets of Sparta itself.

Again, the Theban tactics at Leuctra were not revolutionary, as is usually argued by historians, but simply utilitarian and adapted to Theban national character and its limited strategic ambitions. Indeed, Theban law prescribed only a year's tenure to its generals in the field,

In this sixth-century black-figure vase, light horsemen proudly ride off without armour and shields or even greaves, shoes or heavy helmets, emphasizing their jaunty auxiliary role on the battlefield. But by the fourth century, all armies began to see the need for support troops who could guard hoplites during ever longer marches and retreats, reconnoitre during expeditions, and be lethal in pursuit.

never imagining that any Boeotian army would need to be out of the country for more than twelve months. Nor was the combined employment of Theban horsemen at Leuctra novel. Cavalry had been used earlier in very close concert with infantry at Delium (424), by the Syracusans on Sicily (413), and the Spartans in Asia Minor (395). Moreover, experimentation with phalanx depths greater than the standard eight shields had been common in Greek battle for fifty years, from Delium (424) to Coronea and Nemea (394). And on occasion, superior troops had been placed on the left to knock out the enemy's élite right as at Solygeia (426), Olynthos (382) and Tegyra (375). Rather than a genius, Epaminondas was a keen student of battle tactics, who at Leuctra incorporated, but did not invent, tactical refinements.

On a plate from Rhodes (c. 600) mythical heroes fight as hoplites. Here Hector battles over the body of the fallen Euphorbus. Euphorbus' fate was a common occurrence given the weight of the armour and the confused pushing of the phalanx.

Nor was there even a guarantee that such 'innovations' in themselves were always sound tactically. Deep phalanxes – like columns everywhere – were easily outflanked. It was never guaranteed that additional shields to the rear would always result in commensurate thrusting power, much less compensate for the resulting loss of initial spears in the killing zone. That elusive ratio between depth and breadth at which an army achieved the perfect balance between shield thrusting and initial spear power, between solidarity and flexibility, was never properly solved until Alexander's symphony of multi-faceted light-infantry and cavalry forces.

They surrounded a phalangite column of sixteen men deep, a mass guided by a general who knew the dangers in employing a column of men with vulnerable flanks that also made easy targets for missile attackers. And finally a general on the left of the battle line in theory had no more than a fifty–fifty chance of surviving the collision – an army which wished 'to crush the head of the snake' might just as well in the process lose its own charismatic leader as kill the enemy's.

What Leuctra did demonstrate, however, was that Epaminondas' ideas – if they were in fact his alone (as other generals quickly claimed equal credit for the victory) – were magically suited for a particular time and place in Theban history: highly motivated agrarian troops on the defensive, rallying behind a popular democratic leader and fired by a new sense of political community, were natural ingredients to form a revolutionary column of brawlers. Nine years later at Mantinea (362), however, the same tactics backfired, as Epaminondas himself was killed on the left wing at the moment of triumph, ensuring that the quest for the ultimate knock-out blow against the enemy élite would this time destroy Thebes' rare talent. The death of Epaminondas at Mantinea essentially confined the Theban phalanx to an effective but limited role of protecting the borders of Boeotia – and it is telling that subsequent Greek generals such as Alexander usually led their armies from the right wing, not the left, and with columns sixteen, not fifty, men deep.

Nevertheless, the shocking victory at Leuctra ended the myth of Spartan invincibility and ushered in a decade of Theban hegemony (371–362) in Greece, giving a final radiance to the twilight of hoplite military prowess. After Leuctra, despite opposition from the more conservative board of generals, Epaminondas, in the winter of 370, led more than 40,000 agrarians and their allies on a massive crusade into Laconia itself. And crusade it was, for the Boeotians now were hell-bent on ending for ever, in the only way imaginable, the Spartan threat of invasion – that way being the destruction of the Spartan army in the field and the subsequent liberation of the Messenian helots and Peloponnesian allies from the Spartan yoke. Before Epaminondas, Sparta had invaded the Boeotian countryside on repeated occasions – four times in the prior decade alone; after 370 they never again mounted a serious expedition outside the Peloponnese against anybody. Before Epaminondas, Spartan apartheid in Messenia was unquestioned; after 370 an enormous autonomous city of chauvinistic and bellicose ex-helots loomed across the border. 'Nature,' the Greek orator Alcidamas crowed of the liberation of Messenia, 'has made no man a slave.'

Epaminondas – his life remains mystical, shrouded in second-hand encomia attesting to his selfless character – knew it was now the moment of his agrarian hoplites, free peoples flush with victory and endowed with a sense of their own battlefield invincibility. The infantrymen who followed this remarkable man southward swept aside resistance at the isthmus of Corinth, and shortly reached the outskirts of Sparta itself, ravaging the countryside, thereby demolishing the Spartan boast of perpetually remaining *aporthetos* or 'unplundered'. Plutarch claimed he was the first foreigner in 600 years to invade Laconia. The swollen Eurotas river and the narrowness of the Spartan streets alone saved the Spartans from this possessed northerner who sought to destroy the city itself.

When the Spartan king Agesilaus failed to meet the invaders in a pitched battle, Epaminondas left Sparta, headed back north and then west into Messenia, intent on ruining the material and human fuel for Spartan apartheid – an idea which Liddell Hart once cited as a classic example of 'the grand strategy of indirect approach'. There was now no army in Greece to stop him, and none which cared to if it could. For the Spartans, who sixty years earlier had ravaged the Attic countryside and belittled the Athenians for their 'cowardly' retreat behind their city walls, it was bitter indeed to watch helpless as their own properties were now ransacked by soldiers better than they. More injurious still was the realization that to challenge these ferocious Theban hoplites meant a glorious but sure destruction for the shrinking cadre of Spartiates who had survived the humiliation of Leuctra the previous year.

Declaring Messenia 'free' and autonomous for the first time in almost three centuries, Epaminondas quickly organized the founding of the enormous fortified capital of Messene, from now on the bastion of a free Messenian people who would no longer hand to Sparta either food or men. Modern visitors, who gaze on the elaborate extant fortifications of that citadel on the slopes of Mount Ithome, admire the sophistication of its excavated municipal infrastructure. Should they then travel to the hovels of Classical Sparta, they can appreciate the contrast in cultures – and understand what so terrified the Spartan nation about such an enterprising and energetic people, now at last let loose to exploit for themselves the rich farmland of the Messenian countryside.

In three subsequent invasions during the next decade (368, 366 and 362) Epaminondas applied the same successful strategy of fortification and federation to the Arcadian and Peloponnesian allies, aiding in their ongoing construction of similarly huge and unbreachable walled cities at Megalopolis and Mantinea. These strongholds, along with the now discredited military reputation of the Sparta phalanx, essentially ended for good any notion of Spartan power outside of Laconia. Thanks to Epaminondas, Sparta was surrounded on the outside, and now hollow on the inside; its land had been plundered and its army shamed by refusing battle.

True, after Epaminondas died at Mantinea (362) in the climatic hour of his long-awaited finale with the Spartan phalanx, Theban hegemony gradually faded. But in a larger sense, Epaminondas' magnificent victory at Leuctra, and his daring marches south into the Peloponnesian heartland, resurrected the Hellenic military ideal: free and amateur soldiers, in service to an idea, mustered for a short time, organized for a limited goal, and led by a great man of vision, could outfight professional oligarchs and destroy the entire system of exploitation that so often fields such troops. Like Sherman's army of rural westerners who cut a swath through the heart of the slave-owning South; like Patton's Third Army of American GIs who helped to wreck the Nazi army in its rambunctious march to the Rhine, Epaminondas and his agrarian militiamen who burst into Sparta's land of apartheid were a rare army to remember.

CHAPTER FOUR

The Second Military Revolution (362–336)

The fortifications at Mycenae, along with those at Tiryns, a mile from the bay of Argos, were the most impressive in the entire history of Greece in terms of the sheer thickness of the walls. Scholars are still unsure of the exact relationship between Mycenae and the nearby palace at Tiryns, but it is likely that the two worked in concert rather than in opposition, Tiryns most likely serving as Mycenae's fortified seaport. In general, throughout Greek history walls were antithetical to the culture of a free landed infantry.

Philip of Macedon and the reinvention of Greek warfare

'NOTHING,' THE ORATOR DEMOSTHENES railed at his fourth-century audience of complacent Athenians, 'has been more revolutionized and improved than the art of war. I know,' he continued, 'that in the old times the Spartans, like everyone else, would devote four or five months in the summer to invading and ravaging the enemy's territory with hoplites and citizen militia, and then would go home again. And they were so old-fashioned – or good citizens – that they never used money to buy advantage from anyone, but their fighting was fair and open. On the other hand … you hear of Philip.'

Demosthenes did not mean that Philip had single-handedly crafted a new practice of fighting. Rather, that in the changed climate of Greece in the fourth century, the Macedonian king and his autocratic realm were more innovative, more daring, and more capable of synthesizing into a cohesive whole the various tenets of the new warfare. In a mere century, social status had become almost totally divorced from the Greek battlefield. As the old census rubrics that had once precisely determined the nature of military service gave way, wealthy, middling and poor Greeks could all ride horses, throw javelins or wield the spear, either as hired killers or as reluctant militiamen. Even farmers were employed in the off-season as oarsmen as considerations of class eroded in the face of military utility, and patrollers and light-armed troopers worked out of rural forts and garrisons; but such troops had neither social nor economic affinity, and rarely engaged in pitched battle.

These changes bothered only conservative Greeks of the *polis*, who unlike Philip still clung to the idea that military service meant a mass collision of hoplites, and thus something that transcended killing the enemy in battle. The historian and philosopher Xenophon, for example, complained in his *Ways and Means* that in Athens the hoplite phalanx was losing esteem by recruiting the city's resident aliens into the ranks.

'The *polis* also would be helped,' he advised, 'if citizens proper served alongside one other, and no longer found themselves mixed together with Lydians, Phrygians, Syrians, and barbarians of every type, who form a large portion of our resident alien population.' In contrast, to Philip such a motley throng – 'vagabonds, destitute of means, clad in hides', contemporaries remarked of his recruits – was neither desirable nor repugnant, but only useful to the degree that such men could successfully learn to march, fight, kill, and obey orders. Numbers and skill – not dialect, race, money, status, class or birth – mattered to Philip. In a perverse way, of all generals in the Greek world, the king was the most democratic in his policy of military recruitment, exhibiting a complete absence of the social and cultural snobbery of the old city state.

Who in Greece would support professional troops with regular pay all year round, create a permanent infrastructure sufficient to staff armouries, find timber and metal for military works, and fund engineers, craftsmen and architects to design fortifications and siege engines? Not many and not for long. The very move toward such year-round confrontation in all theatres of the Mediterranean ensured that the vital sources of Greek military revenue – commerce, agriculture, calm in the countryside – would be continually disrupted. Many Greek *poleis*, then, found themselves in a dilemma: they could neither endure provocation and unchecked plundering of their territory, nor afford the necessary permanent force to ensure tranquillity.

Philip's solution was to create a professional army of predators, whose constant military aggression would pay for the costs of its own operation – his troops trained through 35-mile-a-day forced marches without servants or supply wagons. The parochial Greeks still had the relationship between the state and army reversed, as they pondered how to protect their institutions from a variety of new adversaries. But to Philip no such dilemma existed: the state was a mere ancillary to the army, and was therefore organized on the sole principle of providing manpower, labour and capital to ensure that the Macedonian phalanx would be fuelled for further aggrandizement to the south.

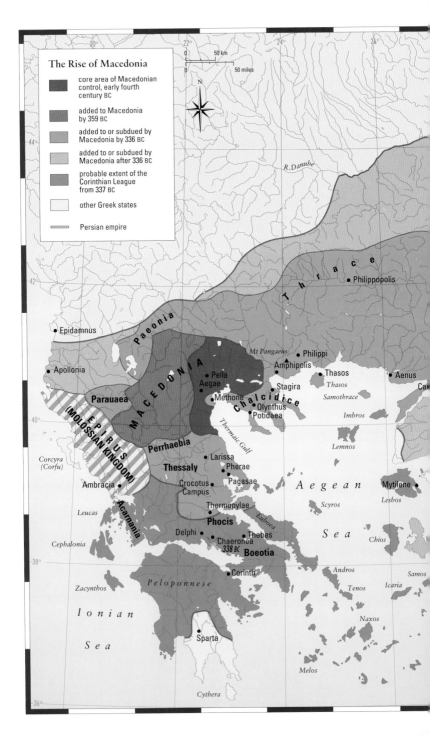

The Rise of Macedonia

- core area of Macedonian control, early fourth century BC
- added to Macedonia by 359 BC
- added to or subdued by Macedonia by 336 BC
- added to or subdued by Macedonia after 336 BC
- probable extent of the Corinthian League from 337 BC
- other Greek states
- Persian empire

0   50 km
0   50 miles

N

R. Danube

T h r a c e

• Philippopolis

P a e o n i a

• Epidamnus

• Apollonia

Parauaea

M
A
C
E
D
O
N
I
A

• Pella
Aegae •
• Methone

Mt Pangaeus
Amphipolis •

• Philippi

Thasos •
Thasos

• Stagira

C h a l c i d i c e
• Olynthus
• Potidaea

Samothrace

Aenus •

Ca

E P I R U S
(MOLOSSIAN KINGDOM)

Corcyra
(Corfu)

Imbros

Perrhaebia

Thermaic Gulf

Lemnos

• Ambracia

Leucas

Thessaly

• Larissa
• Pherae

Crocotus •
Campus

• Pagasae

A e g e a n

Mytilene •

Acarnania

Thermopylae •

Euboea

Scyros

Lesbos

Cephalonia

Phocis

Delphi •
Chaeronea
338 BC

• Thebes

Boeotia

S e a

Chios

Zacynthos

P e l o p o n n e s e

• Corinth

Andros

Samos

Tenos

Icaria

I o n i a n

S e a

• Sparta

Naxos

Melos

Cythera

Even the old constraints of time and space in agrarian warfare were now irrelevant, as Philip's hired killers fought all year round, regardless of terrain, weather or distance. To stop Philip, Greek city states had only three realistic choices: to capitulate, join him, or copy him to such a degree that their culture was no longer a city state at all. Typically they chose none of those options, but instead grandly talked of a utopian Panhellenic alliance that would field a vast force of ships and hoplites for the armageddon to come – the Greek alliance of the Persian wars returned to life in order once more to smash the barbarian from the north. Unfortunately for the Greek city states, the battle-scarred Philip was no enthroned Xerxes, brutal Macedonian pikemen were not gaudy Immortals, and the best defender of the lot, Demosthenes, surely no Themistocles. Thirty thousand phalangites were far more dangerous to Greek liberty than half a million Persians. When the Greeks' anachronistic idea of a dramatic last hoplite stand was finally realized, the dream of another Plataea turned out to be the nightmare of Chaeronea.

In fact, most hoplite militias after the battle of Mantinea (362) rarely fought in decisive pitched battles. Even decades earlier, set battle-pieces were more often replaced by the braggadocio and daring of mercenary captains and itinerant *condotierri*, buccaneers who followed not at all the military protocol of the old Greek *polis*. city states were not averse to hiring thugs and adventurers like Iphicrates, Chabrias, and Chares, whose new peltasts tried to plunder and harass state enemies rather than meet infantry in battle. (Peltasts were light-armed skirmishers, so called because of the small crescent-shaped wicker or leather shields, *peltai*, that they carried, with javelins or short spears, and little if any body armour). Such brigands might loot temples, ransack city treasuries, rob the wealthy, or counterfeit money to keep their troops fed and happy. Military cunning, not courage alone, was what counted. And when they did meet hoplites, they harassed and employed manoeuvre, not shock collision – in that manner, the Athenian Iphicrates had obliterated a company of Spartiate Similars at Corinth in 390, when 250 men were killed. Employing alliance, counter-alliance, subterfuge and plotting, the major players – Athens, Sparta, Thebes, Argos, Corinth, Thessaly and Sicily – used all forces at their disposal to keep an exhausting but nevertheless rough balance of power for the first half of the fourth century, all the while apprehensively eyeing the new threat of Macedon to the north.

Generalship (*stratêgia*) in infantry battle was also changing. Under the city states of the sixth and fifth centuries all commanders fought in or near the front lines, and often perished with their men – their sole duty was to provide a visible courting of danger in the half-hour crash and shove of hoplite battle. In the late fourth century, such heroic leadership would continue – Alexander and Philip were both severely wounded in battle – but Macedonian commanders were now mounted and surrounded at the front by select troops, all the better to give complicated commands by trumpet or personal messenger, to order retreats, feints, and call-ups of reserve contingents.

No one mastered the new possibilities of command better than Philip II of Macedon. The historian Theopompus wrote that Europe had never produced such a man. This was a general, after all, who crucified his opponent, the Phocian Onamarchus, *after* he was killed in battle, and thought nothing of binding 3,000 of the latter's defeated troops and throwing them alive into the sea. Thus appeared the fearful portrait of the limping, one-eyed monster in the conservative fourth-century oratory of the Greek *polis* ('so fond of danger is he, that in order to make his empire greater, he has been wounded in every part of his body while fighting his enemies'), a terrible man who would fight at any time, in all and any manner.

His Macedonian army was big by Greek standards, drawing on the manpower of an enormous and now unified region, enhanced by mercenaries, both Greek and occasionally foreign. Over 30,000 were present at Chaeronea (338) alone, a force beyond the infantry resources of any one *polis*. The size of the Macedonian army ensured numerical superiority over any Greek city state, and Philip was confident that he could bribe, flatter, or threaten individual statesmen in Argos, Thebes, Corinth, Thessaly or the Peloponnese well enough to prevent any lasting coalition that might match his numbers on the battlefield. Since the old Peloponnesian League was long gone, the Athenian empire a dim memory, and the Theban hegemony moribund, there existed no real mechanism to gather or coerce Greek material and human capital for any length of time or at any one place to provide effective resistance in the new manner of war.

His forces were also quick and travelled lightly, as paid mercenaries often do. Without lengthy siege trains or servants, the Macedonian army could appear almost anywhere in mainland Greece in less than a week – a fact known to any blowhard in the assembly who called for the usual lengthy debate about 'preparations' for defence. And in Philip's hands, siegecraft was no longer a matter of months or even years – as the Athenians experienced at Samos (440) and Sicily (415–413), and with the Spartan occupation around Plataea (431–429) – but of mere weeks. His experts, for example, completed a siege of Amphipolis that took less than seventy days; Methone, the Thracian Chalcidice and Pagasae probably fell even more quickly.

The equipment and tactics of his Macedonian phalanx ostensibly did not differ all that radically from the traditional hoplite columns of the Greek city states, though the phalangites were hand-picked as the 'tallest and strongest' of his recruits. The spear, for example, was retained, but lengthened from 8 to nearly 18 feet and more, and fitted with a heavier point and butt. Thus it became a true pike – weighing nearly 15 pounds, more than seven times heavier than the old hoplite spear – which required both hands for adequate control and handling. *Sarissai* were held 6 feet from the butt, and so extended 12 feet in front of the phalangites – giving the Macedonian pikeman an advantage in reach of over 8 to 10 feet more than the traditional hoplite. The round shield became smaller and was hung from the neck or shoulder, as greaves, most breastplates, and heavy headgear were replaced with either leather or composite materials, or abandoned altogether. In addition, the first four or five, not three rows, were now thrusting, giving 40 per cent more spearheads whirling in the killing zone – such a hedgehog-like front provided an unusual degree of offensive might, as well as defensive protection for the unarmoured initial ranks. In general, Macedonian armament was more uniform than the old heterogeneous and privately owned hoplite panoplies – regularized shields and pikes, particular contingents wearing standardized silver ornaments on shields, identical cloaks – all suggesting an unusual degree of militarization, through which the state hired, equipped and in essence now owned the phalangite.

This phalanx of grim, professional 'foot-companions' (*pezetairoi*) fought in concert with the 'companion cavalry' (*hetairoi*), an élite body of aristocratic horsemen, heavily armoured (helmet, breastplate, shoulder guards) with pikes on strong mounts. These horsemen were not showy grandees, but independent tough Macedonian lords in their own right, whose desire was to charge *into* infantry, not around them. Thus, along with lighter-clad Thessalian cavalry, Macedonian horsemen in rhomboid or wedge-shape formation – like 'a flight of cranes' – punched holes in the enemy battle line.

Another contingent of infantry, with better armour and shorter pikes, the 'shield bearers' (*hypaspistai*), also occupied the centre of the Macedonian line, beside the phalangites. The Hypaspists were usually the first infantry forces to follow behind the cavalry onslaught, thereby providing a crucial link between the initial mounted attack and the subsequent follow-up by the phalanx proper. Professional corps of light infantry, slingers, archers and javelin men rounded out the composite army group, supplying both preliminary bombardment and crucial reserve support. And while all these men were mercenaries and in service to an autocratic state, there was an unusual degree of *élan* and *esprit de corps* between princes and the rank-and-file Macedonians, as fighters routinely drank, ate, fought, and played ball among their royal betters. The old civic egalitarianism of the phalanx transmogrified into a brutal camaraderie of sorts so characteristic of even professional troops who fight in column and mass.

Thus this central western idea of fighting decisively *en masse* remained predominant, but Philip brought the terror of such collisions to new heights – a natural experience for his Macedonian rank and file, who were known as thugs by the *polis* Greeks: in Demosthenes' words they were little more than brutes 'who always had their hands on weapons'. Indeed, integrated with, and protected by, variegated light-armed, missile and mounted forces, Philip's phalanx of true pikemen was both more lethal and more versatile than traditional hoplite columns. The Macedonian phalangites could turn their attention exclusively to thrusting their dreadful spears without the cumbersome weight of the old hoplite panoply – much less the need to protect with an enormous shield their immediate citizens on the right.

Offence, pikes and motion forward now counted for everything; defence, large shields and worry over covering hired killers meant little. Used with greater precision and power, the new Macedonian phalanx usually delivered a knock-out blow, once the target had been sighted and then left vulnerable by the work of cavalry and ancillary contingents. Hammer-like, the Macedonian cavalry attacks battered the enemy back on to the clumsy mile-long anvil of the spear-bristling phalanx.

More important, however, Philip brought to western warfare an entirely new ideology of battle. True, the actual stand-up fighting involved frontal assault and so was still every bit as gallant as in the old Greek phalanxes of the past. But warmaking had become much more than personal courage, nerve and physical strength. Nor was killing by Macedonians just over territorial borders. Rather, the strategy of battle was designed predominantly as an instrument of ambitious state policy. Philip's destructive mechanism for conquest and annexation was a radical

In this photograph taken by the author in June 1997 from the acropolis at Chaeronea, the site of the great battlefield of 338 is clearly visible. The small plain of Chaeronea, watered by the Cephissus river, marked the entryway to the vast flatlands of Boeotia, and so served as the ideal bottleneck where Boeotian defenders could marshal a solid line of hoplites between the mountains and thus bar invasion from the north.

source of social unrest and cultural upheaval, not a conservative Greek institution to preserve the existing agrarian community. Philip's territorial ambitions had nothing to do with a few acres outside the *polis*, but rather encompassed a broader vision of mines, harbours, and tribute-paying communities that might be his solely to fuel his rapacious army.

At Chaeronea (338) Philip and his 18-year-old son Alexander broke the phalanx of the Thebans and Athenians and sent Demosthenes scurrying over the hills back to Athens. Greek allied skirmishers, missile troops, horsemen and infantry might have been put to better use in a drawn-out war of attrition and delay, garrisoning passes and ambushing the Macedonian march southward into Greece. Instead, the Greeks in the eleventh hour of their autonomy had marshalled a huge ostentatious force of nearly 30,000 old-style hoplites – precisely the wrong type of army to stop Philip's juggernaut. Predictably and unfortunately for the Greeks, all the elements of the Macedonian tactical renaissance were employed at the battle – a feigned retreat and then sudden onslaught by disciplined phalangites with long pikes, reserve contingents poised to strike at the opportune moment, concerted use of heavy cavalry to exploit gaps in the Greek line, and lightning pursuit to annihilate the defeated.

Against Philip's trained hired killers, the reactionary militiamen of the *polis* had little chance. The various allied contingents, led by Thebes and Athens, had no overall tactical plan; in place of real generals they were led by incompetent political hacks of the old school; and they were completely ignorant of the lethal characteristics of the Macedonian phalanx, which had not yet appeared in a pitched battle in central Greece. The Macedonian pikemen backpedalled, hoping to draw a mad rush by the inexperienced Athenian hoplites. When it came, Philip's professionals stopped on cue, lowered their pikes, and simply impaled the wildly oncoming Athenians. Their idiotic commander Stratocles was still yelling 'On to Macedon' as he led his men to their slaughter. Alexander then rode into the resulting gaps in the Greek line, surrounding the Thebans and herding them from the rear on to the rest of the Macedonian phalangites.

The Thebans' Sacred Band, of course, stayed put on the right, killed to the last man. They were to be interred under the proud stone lion that still stands beside the modern highway – a reminder to the Greeks that about all that brave hoplites could exact from Philip was a limestone beast over their corpses. The hoplite way of fighting was now gone from Greece for ever. Hellenic warfare for nearly the next two centuries was to be almost entirely Macedonian inspired, both in tactics and in technology.

From the century-long experience at the battles of Marathon (490), Plataea (479) and Cunaxa (401), the gallant retreat of the Greek mercenary Ten Thousand (401), and the Spartan experience in Asia Minor (390s), the Greeks had known Persia was vulnerable. Native Hellenic infantry had little difficulty in breaking apart any infantry corps the Persians might field. (Ironically, the chief worry for a Greek expeditionary army in the East was facing the ubiquitous Persian-bought, mercenary hoplites from their own country.) Conquest in the East, then, had been in the mind of many Greek thinkers for generations. The enormous wealth of the Persian empire was especially tempting to Greek politicians, given their own growing economic difficulties, and the accelerating erosion of imperial control across the Aegean in Asia. But the trick for any would-be Greek conqueror of Persia had always been to give up the old idea of a hoplite militia, devising in its place a logistical system and a loyal, unified army from all Greek city states, a social and military amalgam that could be supplied over the great distances to the East, while confronting a variety of enemy troops on any terrain. On the threshold of just such an expedition, Philip was murdered in autumn 336, his professional army passing to his brooding and mostly unbalanced son, whose ideas of the ultimate purposes of military prowess differed substantially from those of his father.

Philip of Macedon, in achieving hegemony over Greece, succeeded beyond the wild imperial expectations of a Darius, Xerxes or Pericles. A military innovator, whose evil genius has been overshadowed by his megalomaniac son, Philip conquered Greece because he had a great army, a propaganda whose time had come – the long postponed punishment and plundering of Persia – and an entirely cynical understanding of the Greek city states. He once remarked that any Greek fortress which could be approached with an ass laden with gold coins could be stormed. He was usually right. The leaders of the *polis*, Philip sensed, while ostensibly preening for the hard, drawn-out task of uniting in opposition to the monster from the north, in private mostly preferred the easier path of a brokered surrender.

The final irony? After launching a technological and tactical revolution that changed the very nature of western warfare, the *polis* Greeks at Chaeronea, at the moment of their destiny, abruptly abandoned a century of innovation and put their faith one last time in the glorious and doomed charge of hoplites – even as the real student of the Greek military renaissance mowed them down, having systematically harvested the fruits of their genius.

WAR AS A SPECIALIZED SCIENCE

Fourth-century Greece is a complex and baffling time of radical change. Civic tragedy and comedy give way on the stage to either the macabre or slapstick. Oratory passes into rhetoric. The road to political absolutism is established as political life becomes paralyzed by factions and subverted by apathy and bribery. The countryside empties of yeomen as farms increase in size even as agricultural science and technique improves. Thus the culture of the old *polis* begins to crystallize along a divide between a professional élite and a new politically impotent peasantry. The result? By the end of the century, a more brutal society – far richer for a few as the monetarization of the economy and new approaches to banking, business and finance create capital undreamed of by the earlier city state, which had frowned on just such commerce and money-lending. The Classical idea of ostracism against the gifted or dangerous was now giving way to the adoration of the powerful through special decree and public bequest. Only in such a larger context can the entire fourth-century revolution in Greek battle practice be understood – a chaotic time when money was for war and war for money.

Nearly every branch of traditional western military science was by the fourth century either reinvented or created from scratch. Siegecraft, which previously had consisted of building walls of circumvallation, mining beneath walls, and the use of crude ladders and ramparts, now centred around the construction of elaborate and multiple battering-rams, wheeled counter-towers that could rival in height the city's ramparts, and the growing ubiquity of catapults and artillery. Whereas the Athenians – the best of the Greek city-stormers – had wasted three years in assaulting Potidaea (432–429), Philip often broke down cities in weeks.

Artillery had been invented on Sicily during the siege of Motya (399) by the engineers of the tyrant Dionysius I and consisted mainly of non-torsion arrow-shooters, resembling medieval crossbows, the so-called 'belly bows' and their larger mobile versions. But some time in the mid fourth century the true torsion catapult came into use. Through the use

MESSENE

Theatre

Stadium

Agora

Messenian Gate

Nearly every Greek city state
was centred around a fortified hill,
which usually marked the site of the
original town. But unlike either Mycenaean
citadels or Near Eastern palaces, the Greek acropolis
was a centre for civic, religious and financial operations.
Citizens not only walked up to temples to worship the
patron deity of the polis, they might also inspect financial
records of their municipality, view the capital reserves of
the state, and store state-owned weaponry. There were no
imperial residences or monumental tombs on the
acropolis; but in time of deepest peril when the outer
walls had been reached, the 'high city' might offer the last
chance of die-hard resistance.

Arcadian Gate

Altar of Zeus

ACROPOLIS

Temple of Artemis

pring

M o u n t   I t h o m e

Laconian Gate

N

The walls of Messene
here pictured went up in the
winter of 369 after Epaminondas
invaded the heartland of Sparta and
then proceeded over the mountains to
liberate the helots of Messenia. The
enormous fortifications made use of the
slopes of Mount Ithome and were
designed to envelop enough open land
for the inhabitants to bring in livestock
and to cultivate sizable gardens.

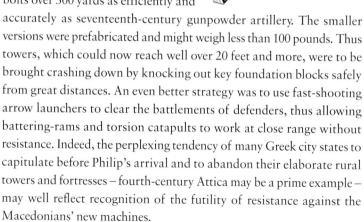

The lithobolos *('stone-caster') represented the climax of Greek mathematical science married to practical engineering. The largest models could heave stones nearly 200 pounds in weight, and could cast small objects over 300 yards.*

of springs and winches, human hair – the ancient trade in women's locks was to become enormous – was twisted and cocked, and propulsive power thus stored. On release such machines might hurl stones or specially crafted bolts over 300 yards as efficiently and accurately as seventeenth-century gunpowder artillery. The smaller versions were prefabricated and might weigh less than 100 pounds. Thus towers, which could now reach well over 20 feet and more, were to be brought crashing down by knocking out key foundation blocks safely from great distances. An even better strategy was to use fast-shooting arrow launchers to clear the battlements of defenders, thus allowing battering-rams and torsion catapults to work at close range without resistance. Indeed, the perplexing tendency of many Greek city states to capitulate before Philip's arrival and to abandon their elaborate rural towers and fortresses – fourth-century Attica may be a prime example – may well reflect recognition of the futility of resistance against the Macedonians' new machines.

Defensive engineers were not idle in the face of rapid breakthroughs in siegecraft and artillery, and most of the really impressive city-circuits – Mantinea, Megalopolis and Messene – and rural forts on the frontier of Attica, Megara and in the Argolid were constructed in just this period of the early and mid fourth century. The chief improvements consisted of a systematic use of isodomic ashlar blocks, binding courses, embrasures, internal tressing, more extensive foundations, and drafted corners to ensure wall stability at vastly increased heights and breadths. Forts were framed with towers over 30 feet in height that housed small anti-personnel non-torsion catapults to prevent besiegers from approaching too near the circuits. Some of the embrasure windows were equipped with elaborate shuttering systems designed to open and close as wheeled catapults put down continuous fire.

Yet by the mid third century, besiegers were fielding enormous catapults whose torsion designs could hurl stones over 150 pounds in weight, making the new taller towers increasingly vulnerable to blows at their bases. The necessity of having long stocks and powerful frames meant that torsion catapults would always be more easily manned from the ground than from high up on ramparts and towers.

In this new arms race, engineers in turn ingeniously designed circuits to follow the natural defensive contours of the terrain, and sophisticated sally ports were built with the idea of sudden mounted sorties. Still, just as the walled defence had remained pre-eminent in the fifth century, so in the fourth the momentum radically swung the other way to the attacker. Even the most elaborately constructed garrisons were never really safe from engineers as sophisticated as Philip's and Alexander's. Again, the key was cost; despite the enormous expenditures needed to create and transport artillery, and to construct wheeled towers and rams, fortifications were even more expensive. Only the largest cities – Rhodes, Megalopolis, Salamis on Cyprus – had the capital to craft adequate protection and to store enough provisions to withstand even a short siege.

Prior to the late fifth century, light-armed troops and missile-throwers were relegated to minor roles in battle – such men could not charge hoplites. Their missiles were often ineffective against bronze plate. They usually owned little if any property. Their slings, bows and javelins required training beyond the amateur ideal of the hoplite; and the most effective shooters were from the margins – Rhodes, Crete, Thrace and Scythia – of the Greek world. The thousands of non-hoplites present at the battle of Plataea (479) played little role in the fighting, and by 424 Athens still had no formal corps of such light infantry. This all changed in the fourth century, however, when military service became divorced from civilian status, manpower was for hire, and the phalanx no longer mustered exclusively on flat plains, but was to fight in transit over the mountains and defiles of Greece and Persia.

Stone-throwers are known as early as Homer, and appear haphazardly in Classical history as the poorest of troops who collect random rocks and small stones to pelt infantry before running away. Their efficacy was minimal, but the combination of sling and lead bullet was an entirely different story altogether. Such specialists from Achaea, the Balearic islands and Thessaly came into their own in the fourth century, when deployed in front of and behind infantry, depending on the particular stage of fighting. Thus the best of such troops – the Rhodians apparently commanded the highest prices – were hired on the Athenian campaign in Sicily, accompanied the Ten Thousand into Persia, and were customarily always part of Philip's entourage.

With lifelong training, seasoned slingers might cast lead bullets over 350 yards, shattering the bones of any exposed limbs and faces of heavy infantry and forcing archers to retreat out of range. While the Spartans had complained on Sphacteria that enemy missile troops killed good and bad troops alike, thus ending the heroic role of personal bravery, in the fourth century that anonymity was precisely the point – as Philip himself learned when he fell victim to his own military revolution, losing his eye to a slinger's bullet, while his son Alexander the Great was nearly killed at the siege of Gaza by a catapult bolt to the shoulder. No surprise that when old King Archidamus of Sparta (c. 360) heard of a new catapult, he lamented, 'Man's martial valor is of no value any more.'

Archery was not important in Greece before the fourth century. Good bows were difficult to manufacture and remained fragile – often carried in special cases to prevent their glued components from weathering and disassembling. And to shoot the composite bow required extraordinary arm and upper-body strength. After ten or so volleys at maximum pull, the archer could not maintain his distance, accuracy, or a rapid rate of fire. Moreover, the introduction of the hoplite's plate armour usually reduced the vulnerability of the target; most bronze helmets and corselets offered ample protection to turn arrows. So against large shields and upraised spears of later massed foot soldiers, salvoes from the bow could not break oncoming armoured infantry. And most bowmen could only get a couple of minutes' worth of ten or twenty volleys before running hoplites closed the 200 yards of vulnerable no man's land.

But just as importantly, western infantry found no social or cultural advantages in archery. Bowmen relied on individual skill; they fought solitarily, and were neither trained in hand-to-hand combat, nor eager to inflict and withstand shock. Manoeuvre, speed, deception, patience and evasion were inherent in the entire mentality of archery training and tactics. In contrast, the military ideology of the Classical Greeks was

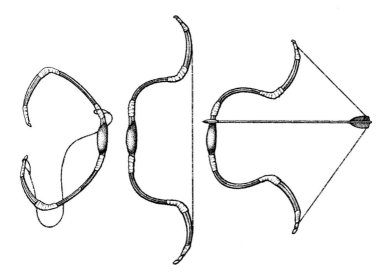

The so-called composite bow was glued and cured from wood and horn, and described by the early Greeks as palintonos, 'back-springing'. The famous scene in Homer's Odyssey, where the returning hero and his son alone can string the family's bow, is a clear reference to a composite model. In theory, a good archer could hit targets 300 yards away. In fact, he could shoot accurately at up to only 150 yards. After a few volleys, exhaustion would set in, lessening his effective range. Thus armoured hoplites who could lumber 150–200 yards in less than three minutes were rarely stopped by archery attack.

originally predicated on precisely the opposite criteria: group solidarity and instantaneous brute force of amateur militias who found their success in their own degree of muscular strength, nerve and loyal dependence to like kind. Equally important, western armies fought over property – the conquest and occupation of farmland or city walls – where obstacles, both human and inanimate, had to be 'pushed' aside through sheer force. Bowmen could kill and maim at a distance, but by themselves they were often unable to take and hold ground.

So throughout early Greek literature of the city state, the man with the bow is relegated to the fringes of the battlefield, a savage, tribalist, or worse. When archers were needed for foreign campaigning they, like slingers, were usually recruited from outside the Greek world of the *polis* – often in the backwaters of Crete and Macedonia, or even Scythia and Persia. Early Greek communities purportedly outlawed the use of missiles altogether. Beginning with the *Iliad*, there is a constant refrain in Greek poetry and history that the bow is both effeminate ('womanly')

After the victories at Marathon and Plataea, Persians on the run or in their death throes were popular topics of red-figure vase painters. Their leather helmets, fabric shirts and pants, and the ubiquitous gortyos, *which held their bow and arrows, offered dramatic contrast to hoplites' full body armour, spears, and exposed arms and legs. By the time Alexander invaded Asia in 334, most Greeks had grown accustomed to such pictorial propaganda for over 150 years, and thus considered Asiatic soldiers effeminate.*

and oriental ('barbarian'). From Aeschylus, Herodotus, Euripides and Thucydides we learn that the Greeks felt that its use was somehow unfair, and put the hero on par with the coward, should anonymous bolts from the sky kill all alike. Death from 'cowardly arrows' was an ignominious end for a hoplite. There was something entirely un-Hellenic about the idea that a man could kill at a distance without danger to himself, an act naturally more suited for barbarians and the poor.

But once western armies ventured from their own terrain, their deficiency in archery was dangerously apparent and their former reluctance to diversify their arsenal by the fourth century revealed as parochial and foolish. When Xenophon's Ten Thousand or Alexander's Macedonians went East they were obliged to hire bowmen to protect their armies in transit and to cover stationary phalanxes as they prepared to charge. Thus, as in the case of slingers, bowmen found greater opportunity in the fourth century in the open mercenary market. Now they were to become an integral part of combined arms and no longer represented either a social or cultural affront to infantry.

Some city states had always brought along their unarmoured poor – as 'light-armed' or 'naked' troops who skirmished with missiles before and after the hoplite crash, and then joined in during retreat and pursuit. But by the fifth century, more specialized Thracian peltasts began to be hired by Greek armies to deal with non-hoplite enemies. And by the end of the century, some city states were equipping their own such troops as both mobile javelin-throwers and spearmen, who could dash around the flanks of heavy infantry, charging, stabbing or releasing javelins, and then retreating. On Pylos (425) and again at Corinth (390) such troops nearly annihilated traditional Spartan hoplite infantry. Philip took note of these more agile fighters, and the lighter armour and greater fluidity of his Macedonian phalangites may have had its genesis in an effort to blend the offensive thrust and solidarity of hoplites with the mobility and quickness of peltasts.

Hoplite snobbery also had ramifications on the opposite end of the social scale. Since the Dark Ages, élite horsemen represented dangerous aristocrats, who needlessly let horses pasture when their land might be better used for intensive farming or livestock grazing. There was a western general taboo against eating horses, and without adequate harnesses they were far less effective draft animals than yoked oxen. Moreover, to feed a single horse for a year cost more than maintaining a family of six; and the price of a horse was about eighteen months of a day-labourer's wages – and over three times more than the hoplite panoply. Not surprisingly, in every right-wing *putsch* in the history of Athenian democracy, horsemen were at the centre of the reactionary conspiracy, and were generally despised by yeoman infantry. In most Greek expeditions they numbered little more than 5 per cent of the total combatants.

Such seigniors always were relatively ineffective chargers against the spears of armoured and massed hoplites; riders mounted small ponies of less than 10 hands (a little over 3 feet) at the withers, on saddle cloths

Chariots had stopped being used for military purposes during the Mycenaean period. The scythed chariots of the Persians were mostly a terror weapon that inflicted little real damage to Alexander's phalangites and hypaspists, who either parted on cue, or covered their bodies with their shields. When the Greeks and Romans ventured overseas they were startled at the appearance of chariots in Cyrenae and Britain, which they felt were of little value and thus wisely had long since been superseded in their own military practice.

without stirrups. Yet by the fourth century, there were targets for cavalry other than an immovable line of spearmen, and the social censure against equestrians was vanishing with the erosion of agrarianism and census classifications. Increasingly, as in the case of lighter armed foot soldiers and missile troops, horsemen – predominantly from Boeotia, Thessaly and Macedon – were now used more frequently to ride down poorly arranged infantry, and were vital for pursuit and reconnaissance.

Philip saw that with proper armour for horse and rider, and pike instead of javelin or sword, a corps of heavy cavalry would be invaluable in two vital roles: first, at opportune moments charging suddenly into gaps between various contingents of Greek hoplites where they might sow disorder on poorly protected sides and backs (as Alexander accomplished brilliantly at Chaeronea in 338); and second, riding right into the ranks of poorly armoured eastern infantry. Trained mounted lords from the estates of Macedon might trample over Persian mercenaries, and send shock waves of psychological distress far out of proportion to their actual numerical presence on the battlefield. Horsemen, of course, could still not anchor Greek armies when it was a question of fighting other Greek armies. But against easterners, the royal Macedonian idea of heavy cavalry élites proved invaluable at tearing gaps through foot soldiers.

There is also a larger explanation – paradoxical as it may appear – for this fourth-century Greek renaissance in the science of killing people. The continual progress in western military practice derives in large part from its larger liberal tradition of free speech, unbridled investigation and continual intellectual controversy – all endeavours relatively free from state censorship or religious stricture and very much alive still in the fourth-century twilight of the autonomous *polis*. Thus tactical and strategic doctrine, technological innovation and logistical and organizational reform functioned in that same free-wheeling sphere, and have in the West all been analyzed, argued, questioned – even attacked – at symposia and in publication, regardless of state boundaries or even at times more parochial national interests.

Such reasoned inquiry – in the context of killing dare we call it the dividend of the Greek enlightenment? – ensures that western warfare is volatile. It changes constantly. The prior year's success is instantly criticized by the armchair intellectual, battle veteran and pragmatic engineer alike, all eager and willing to challenge, both in person and in writing, the blinkered conservatism of the more professional military mind. In a free society and economy, money, land, fame, power and influence often go to the man who discovers a catapult or masters the science of logistics. God, the king, the peeping court toady or venerable ancestors do not veto military innovation out of religious, political or cultural concerns. Inquiry into war is not a part of or subservient to either government or religion, much less spiritual growth and harmony. Neither is the dissemination of military research confined to a small cloister nor is the abstract knowledge of arms kept from the reading public.

Thus a Greek's advice succeeded or failed solely by its logic and its degree of efficacy on the battlefield. It was neither hindered nor enhanced by extraneous religious or philosophical doctrine. Compare other traditions of military scholarship. The great Chinese military strategist Sun-tzu is sometimes cryptic, often mystical, and always part of some larger religious paradigm. His very first page reads: 'The Tao causes the people to be fully in accord with the ruler. Thus they will die with him; they will live with him and fear danger. Heaven encompasses yin and yang, cold and heat, and the constraints of the seasons. Earth encompasses far or near, difficult or easy, expansive or confined, fatal or tenable terrain.'

Contrast the matter-of-fact tone and spirit found on the corresponding opening page from a roughly contemporary Greek military treatise of the fourth century, Aeneas the Tactician's *On the Defense of Fortified Positions*: 'The arrangement of the troops is to be accomplished with reference to both the size of the state and the topography of the town, its sentries and patrols, and any other services for which troops are required in the city – it is in view of all these factors that one must take up the assignments.' Aeneas' singular purpose is to instruct on *how to prevent a city from being stormed*. Period. If you want to take a city, not please the emperor or god, not learn about yourself, Aeneas is the better guide. That autonomous and intellectually independent legacy of formal military science – crucial to the successful warmaking of western armies – had its origins in Greece and the later Hellenistic world.

The agrarian hoplite protocols of seventh- to fifth-century Greece had tended to stifle military innovation. Technology, tactics, strategy and ruse were all antithetical to the hoplite–farmer's notions of a day's war of colliding phalanxes, and there is a rich literary tradition of city state Greeks railing against arrows, missiles, artillery and walls as threats to battle heroism. But during the later fifth century, two phenomena – one political, the other intellectual – conspired to end that military stasis, to complicate warfare, and thus to bring the 'science' of killing thousands into the mainstream of the Greek intellectual tradition.

First, as we have seen, the erosion of the old agrarian Greek *polis* in the aftermath of the calamitous Peloponnesian war allowed a variety of new forces and technologies to emerge – all free from sanctimonious agricultural stricture. Mercenaries, artillery, cavalry and marines were by the fourth century practicable military options, requiring not merely a fighting battle-commander of muscle and nerve, but a real thinking general to worry about reserves, articulation and manoeuvre. New sciences such as logistics, encampment, siegecraft and the permanent occupation and administration of captured land required both theoretical and applied expertise.

Second, Greek contemporary intellectual fervour was dominated by Platonic and sophistic thought. The philosophers and rhetoricians of the late fifth century were not always utopian, but rather often singularly pedagogical and utilitarian, seeking concretely – and usually for pay – to apply dialectic, language and induction to a plethora of practical topics: agriculture, medicine, natural science, politics – and, of course, war. Military affairs – generalship (*stratêgika*), the arrangement of troops (*taktika*) and weapons training – were a category of this systematized approach to learning, and thus became a natural and important part of the Greek philosophical movement which had grown ever more practical.

War was not a question of bravery or a reflection of values, but simply an art (*technê*) like any other.

Xenophon (428–354) is the best example of this mixture of battlefield experience and philosophical training. In some sense, he stands as the founder of the military intellectual tradition in the West. Veteran of a wide variety of campaigns in Greece and Persia and follower of Socrates, Xenophon wrote handbooks such as *The Cavalry Commander* and *On Horsemanship* and he discussed generalship, tactics and strategy in his *Memorabilia*, *Oeconomicus*, and *Education of Cyrus*. In these treatises Xenophon draws on his own practical experiences as a mercenary leader among the Ten Thousand, and as a close friend of the Spartan king Agesilaus, seeking, in a systematic, logical way, improvement in existing Greek military practice. Even if Xenophon himself was not widely read by the soldiers in the ranks, his work suggests that such topics were the fourth-century rage of both *polis* leaders and professional mercenary captains – indeed he mentions contemporary 'professors of tactics', itinerants who peddled their expertise to the highest bidder. We get a rather contemptuous picture of such would-be experts in Plato's *Ion*, in which rote knowledge about military affairs is not considered real wisdom.

Xenophon's contemporary, the pragmatic Aeneas the Tactician (*c*. 360), follows in the same utilitarian tradition. His apparently vast *Military Preparations* is lost, but an extant monograph, *How to Survive Under Siege,* covers everything from the mundane (e.g. passwords, reveille, codes, tunnelling) to the broader employment of mercenaries, sorties and plans of evacuation.

Unfortunately, almost all the late fourth- and third-century followers of Xenophon and Aeneas – and others who probably wrote similarly practical military handbooks – are mere names, their work lost. Worse yet, the subsequent enormous industry of Hellenistic military scholarship (nearly thirty names of such authors and titles are known to us) has likewise been obliterated. Yet these third- and second-century tacticians and strategists – Cinemas, Apollonius, Pyrrhus, and dozens of others now forgotten – marked the ancient high point of military inquiry. Their pragmatic treatments of phalanx tactics, ballistics, fortification and siegecraft must have disseminated military innovation among a growing military intelligentsia, and so contributed to the ever-growing complexity of Hellenistic warfare. The handbooks of Ctesibus (*c.* 270), for example, provided the technical know-how for catapult construction, and founded the entire mathematical science of calibration and propulsion as it applied to artillery. The dissemination of his work in the later *Belopoeicae* of both Philo (*c.* 200) and Heron (*c.* 70) aided the mass construction of catapults throughout the Classical world.

After the Roman conquest of Greece in the late second century, Greek military writing became somewhat more dry, philosophical, and often pedantic. Centuries of world government and the supremacy of the Roman legion obviated the need for radical new thinking on the battlefield. The polymath philosopher and historian Posidonius of Apamea (135–50) reflects the new historical realities, and so he seems (his work is lost) to have transformed the vibrant Greek tradition of practical, hands-on military research into abstract philosophical speculation about distant and largely forgotten (Greek) military formation and arrangement. All surviving military writing, unfortunately, draws from Posidonius' work. And so the extant *Tactics* of Asclepiodotus (*c.* 100), Aelian (*c.* AD 100–110), Arrian (*c.* AD 140) and Onasander's *The General* (*c.* AD 50) offered little of value about ongoing Roman military practice, providing the military historian, past and present, with no novel insight on the actual conduct of either past Greek or contemporary Roman armies.

The second and final phase of western war was now complete. If the Classical age had radically altered warfare through the unique idea of decisive battle, in which free men crafted conflict as a decisive face-to-face collision of shock troops, so the fourth century ushered in the logical conclusion to the entire Greek discovery of decisive engagement: total and absolute fighting as a natural extension of social and economic life. To accompany the earlier discovery of a civic militia which preferred

instantaneous results, the entire Greek genius for unfettered inquiry and expression would now be turned to its last horizon of inquiry – the science of killing people. The tragedy – and the legacy which we still today bear in the West – is that the former invention of decisive battle led to a diminution in the number killed and an ethical brake on both the length and the arena of war; yet the latter revolution accomplished just the opposite, and therefore taught the West that decisive battle is not the culmination of warfare, but rather a very effective instrument in the wider effort to destroy the enemy entirely.

Nike (Victory) appeared almost everywhere in Greek art – on vases, as statues and pedimental sculpture, incised on bronze armour, and stamped on coins – signifying the Greeks' near constant warmaking and their sense that victory was impossible without the presence of a deity. Usually, she is portrayed with flowing robes, two to four wings, and often with a shield and spear. Because the victors rarely took many casualties in traditional Greek battles – less than 5 per cent of their original force – and almost none at all against the Persians – as the few hundred dead at Marathon, Plataea, and Alexander's victories attest – Nike was seen as a beautiful young woman, whose sudden alighting to the pious army brought it life, prosperity and honour.

CHAPTER FIVE

Alexander the Great and the Creation of Hellenistic Warfare (335–146)

Before Alexander the Great it was rare to see portraits of famous Greek generals displayed publicly. Indeed, notables such as the Spartan regent Pausanias, Miltiades, the Greek victor at Marathon, Pericles and Alcibiades at one time or another were severely criticized for efforts at bringing public attention to themselves, or claiming individual credit for the victories of their particular city states. As acceptance of his godhead grew, Alexander realized the propaganda value of displaying his youthful countenance, and within a few years of the start of his reign, statues appeared in the many thousands from Athens to the Indus, all sharing the prerequisite characteristics: flowing hair, lithe though muscular physique, and gaze transfixed at the upper horizon, as if pondering further conquest and good deeds for the brotherhood of man.

Marching through Asia

THE FACTS, THOUGH NOT the assessment, of Alexander's decade-long march through Asia are generally beyond dispute. Within two years of his ascension to the Macedonian kingship in the autumn of 336, Alexander, through murder and military force, eliminated all dynastic rivals and secessionary monarchs. He ended for good the old idea of politically autonomous Greek city states, levelling Thebes as a warning to idealistic, nostalgic statesmen like Demosthenes. He then invaded Asia Minor in 334, and after the victories at Granicus (334) and Issus (333), everything west of the Euphrates river was his for the taking. The brutal conquest of Tyre and Gaza and the acquisition of Egypt itself cemented his southern flank. And after his victory at Gaugamela in the autumn of 331, the eastern satrapies and client states of Persia were without protection from Alexander's onslaught. After a further five years of brutal subjugation of indigenous tribes and nomads in eastern Iran, Afghanistan and Bactria, he marched east of the Indus and defeated the Indian Raja Porus at the Hydaspes, marking the eastern limit of his global campaigning.

Within a decade he had destroyed the Persian empire, brought Greeks 3,000 miles to the east, created a veneer of Hellenic culture in his path, and left a lethal military machine in the hands of his seasoned marshals, dour realists eager to carve up his spoils. At 33 Alexander died; alcoholic, weakened by malaria and old battle wounds, and very probably poisoned by his own increasingly terrified associates.

To understand the warmaking of Alexander the Great, we must first appreciate the 21-year-old's decision in September 335 to erase from the collective memory of Greece the entire city of Thebes – in many ways the most illustrious *polis* in Hellenic history. The people of Thebes had rebelled against Philip's league of Greek states in the hope that the young Alexander was either dead himself or too inexperienced to stop them. Their destruction was no aberration, but simply a foretaste of the entire Alexandran approach to military practice so successful later in Asia. The ultimatum of surrender, the preference of lethal force to negotiation, the subsequent obliteration of the enemy, the inevitable murder of women and children and razing of house and home, the dire warning to do the same to other would-be insurrectionists, and always the dramatic and mythic flair to mask the barbarity: in the case of Thebes the sparing of the poet Pindar's house to emphasize his Hellenism – all were part of the feigned reluctance to murder the innocent. Alexander understood as few others that a cultural veneer was vital to the practice of western war if it was not to appear merely as extermination.

After the assassination of Philip in 336 and the subjugation of the Greek states following the destruction of Thebes, the 20-year-old Alexander began his deceased father's planned Persian invasion with a victory at the Granicus river near the Hellespont (333). In his first savage onslaught at the Granicus, Alexander established a pattern of battle in which we can distinguish a rough sequence of events that appears at all three of his subsequent major triumphs at Issus (333), Gaugamela (331) and the Hydaspes (326): first, brilliant adaptation to often unfavourable terrain (all his battles were fought on or near rivers); second, generalship by frightful example of personal – and always near-fatal – courage at the head of the companion cavalry; third, stunning cavalry blows focused on a concentrated spot in the enemy line, horsemen from the rear then turning the dazed enemy on to the spears of the advancing phalanx; and finally, subsequent pursuit or destruction of enemy forces in the field, reflecting Alexander's impulse to eliminate, not merely to defeat, hostile armies.

Macedonians, unlike earlier Greeks or contemporary Persians, usually carried their own provisions and panoply, servants packing only essential food and other camp material. Absent was the later long baggage train of wagons, women and livestock. 'When Philip organized his first army,' wrote Frontinus, the first-century AD military compiler, 'he ordered that no one was to use a wagon. The horsemen he allowed one servant each, but for the infantry he permitted for every ten men one attendant only, who was charged with carrying milling equipment and ropes. When the army went out during the summer, each man was ordered to carry thirty days' provisions on his back.'

Local officials were usually forced to supply caches of food in advance – emptying the countryside of food for a 60-mile radius – allowing Alexander's sleek army to hop from one depot to another. 'Philip,' wrote the military rhetorician Polyaenus of the Roman era, 'made the Macedonians march 300 stadia [about 34 miles], bearing their arms and carrying as well helmets, greaves, spears, provisions and their daily utensils.'

The enormous apparatus of travelling markets was inimical to the Macedonians' prime directive of speed, rapid onslaught, and decisive quick blows. The Macedonian army travelled in the manner it attacked, and thus logisticians, quartermasters, and financial planners in the shadows were the unheralded geniuses that made the entire terrifying onslaught work; no army before or after was so finely organized and so independent of lengthy support trains and camp followers. Yet to support Alexander's army for a single day – infantry, cavalry, support troops, baggage and pack animals – over 250 tons of grain and forage alone were required, and over 70,000 gallons of water. And on at least some occasions when it was impossible to live off the land or find

Alexander's Empire

- Philip II's possessions, 336 BC
- Alexander's empire, 323 BC
- allegiance to Alexander
- Persian royal road
- route of Alexander and his generals (334–323 BC)
- march of the 'Ten Thousand' (401–400 BC)
- Agesilaus in Asia Minor (396–323 BC)
- battle, with date
- city founded by Alexander

accessible water, more than 1,000 tons of supplies were carried and consumed each day. At Gaza alone, his troops needed 6 million gallons of water to supply them for the two-month siege – most of it inaccessible from local sources, and thus probably imported at great distances by land and sea.

The immediate legacy of Alexander the Great? Other than tactical and logistical brilliance, not much. To his contemporaries, Alexander in the years after his death was, to be frank, little more than an ingenious boy and impetuous front-line fighter who had run wild for a decade and left a rich source of booty for wiser and older men like Seleucus, Antipater, Antigonus and Ptolemy to haggle over and divide up. The Greeks on the mainland mostly rejoiced at his death. Alexander's half-educated infatuation with eastern mysticism, and play-acting at divinity failed to impress Philip's old guard of Macedonian veterans, who finally tired of the antics of this rather dangerous alcoholic. Indeed, it was not until the reign of Augustus that Alexander – the propagandistic potentialities of his hero worship for any would-be world conqueror were obvious – was seen in his now familiar role of Alexander Magnus.

Extant ancient historians of the Roman Age, their sources traceable in a convoluted trail back to contemporaries of Alexander himself, present both a 'good' and 'bad' Alexander – either an Achilles come alive whose youthful exuberance and piety brought Hellenism to its proper limits, or a megalomaniac, drunken and indulgent thug, who butchered most in his path before turning on his father's friends and compatriots, the very men whose loyalty and genius created him in the first place. That debate continues today. But if we put aside later romance about Alexander – his supposed efforts to achieve 'The Brotherhood of Mankind' or to bring 'civilization' to the barbarians – we can at least agree that his real distinction is entirely military: a shrewd appraisal both of the destructiveness of western arms, and the political, cultural and economic arts that were needed in order to use such power without restraint.

TOTAL WAR

Before his apotheosis as warrior-god, Alexander at first claimed that his mission eastward was both Hellenic and warranted: he was, first, to free the Asiatic Greeks from Persian satraps; second, to provide the muscle for the lofty ideal of Panhellenism by uniting the squabbling Greek *poleis* into a national federation on the mainland; and third, to punish the Persians for Xerxes' invasion of Greece 150 years before and for their burning of the Athenian acropolis. Alexander accomplished all three ostensible goals through undeniable military genius and gratuitous slaughter. But his real purpose was largely the quest for personal glory and theft on a continental scale. In the place of an eroding imperial Persian kleptocracy, he left behind fragmented but exploitive Greek monarchies, whose military dynamism was devoted mostly to enriching a tiny élite.

To Alexander the strategy of war meant not the defeat of the enemy, the return of the dead, the construction of a trophy and the settlement of existing disputes, but rather, as his father had taught him, the annihilation of all combatants and the destruction of the culture that had dared to field such opposition to his imperial rule. Thus Alexander's revolutionary practice of total pursuit and destruction of the defeated enemy ensured battle casualties unimaginable just a few decades earlier. At the Granicus river in May 334 Alexander destroyed the Persian army outright, surrounded the trapped Greek mercenaries, and massacred all except 2,000 whom he sent back in chains to Macedon. Our sources disagree over the precise casualty figures, but Alexander may have exterminated between 15,000 and 18,000 Greeks *after* the battle was essentially won – killing more Hellenes in a single day than the entire number that had fallen to the Mede at Marathon, Thermopylae, Salamis and Plataea combined. In his first battle to liberate the Greeks, it turned out that Alexander had killed more of them than all the Persian kings combined in over a century and a half of trans-Aegean campaigning. Perhaps as many as 20,000 Persians fell as well at Granicus – casualty figures themselves far higher than in any single hoplite battle in two centuries of warfare on the mainland.

The next year at Issus, against the grand army of Darius III himself, the cumulative totals of war dead reached new magnitudes. Perhaps another 20,000 Greek mercenaries fell and anywhere from 50,000 to 100,000 Persian recruits were dead by the end of the day – a formidable challenge of time and space to butcher for eight hours more than 300 men every minute. This was now western warfare taken to new heights of extermination. The phalanx did not push men off the battlefield as much as slaughter them from the rear. In the space of a year, Alexander had killed more Greeks in two engagements than had fallen in the entire history of pitched battle among the city states – and he was only beginning.

Alexander's subsequent victory at Gaugamela probably resulted in another 50,000 being killed outright – we need not believe inflated casualty figures of over a quarter of a million. A few thousand more Greek mercenaries also fell. Most of the enemy were trampled or speared in the rout, from Alexander's novel practice of pursuit until exhaustion – on the keen understanding that the key in battle was now to destroy all combatants, lest they re-form to meet him on the inevitable battlefield to come.

At his fourth and last battle victory over the Indian prince Porus at the Hydaspes river in 326 Alexander killed around 20,000 of the enemy. Very conservative figures suggest that in the space of just eight years Alexander the Great had slain well over 200,000 men in pitched battle alone, *over 40,000 of them Greeks*. Thus while we may marvel at the tactical genius of Alexander the Great in ensuring the victory and safety of his own men, we must also acknowledge that the success of his Macedonian army was due to its constant drilling, endless campaigning, considerable experience in pitched battles – and ultimately its revolutionary ability and desire to shatter the enemy, break its formation, and then butcher the unarmed and fleeing to the point of annihilation. To Alexander the more men he killed now, the fewer he would face later.

In between these formal battles, Alexander stormed a host of both Greek and Persian cities. As with battlefield casualties, exact figures for the dead are disputed, but reasonable inferences – given the additional populations of women, children and the aged – suggest far more were slain than all the combatants in his four previous formal battles put together. As a rule of thumb, we should assume that Alexander systematically captured and often enslaved all cities in his path, beginning in Asia Minor, proceeding to the Syrian coast, then into the eastern satrapies of Persia and ending with the carnage of Indian communities in the Punjab. We hear little from any sources about the precise number of those killed in Alexander's capture of Miletus (334), Halicarnassus (334), Sagalassus (333), Pisidia (333), Celanae (333), Soli (333), the massacre of the Branchidae (329), the various fortresses of Syr-Darya (329), the stronghold of Ariamazes (328), the Indian cities of Massaga (327), Aornus (327) and Sangala (326). Most of these strongholds were larger than Thebes, his inaugural siege, which saw 6,000 Greeks butchered in the streets. Occasionally we read in our sources of anecdotes about gratuitous executions and crucifixions should Alexander have been frustrated in the siege or suffered a minor wound in the assault. The historian Arrian, for example, at one point suggested 80,000 were butchered in the storming of the southern Punjabi cities around Sindimana and mentions 17,000 Indians killed and 70,000 captured at Sangala. I would think it a very conservative estimate to assume that a quarter of a million urban residents were massacred outright between 334 and 324, most of them civilian defenders who unfortunately lived in the path of Alexander's trek east.

The most notorious and well-documented carnage, however, was at Tyre and Gaza. After months of heroic defence, Tyre fell on 29 July 332. Most military historians emphasize only the brilliance and tenacity of the Macedonian besiegers, forgetting that their engines and science were simply the means to an end – in this case, the murder of innocents. We have no exact record of how many were lost in the city's

GAUGAMELA PHASE I

In late September 331, Alexander met Darius III in the northern Tigris valley at Gaugamela, a small village not far from Arbela to force the decisive battle for the Persian empire. Alexander had collected his largest force ever, but it was still under 50,000 men, and perhaps five times smaller than the Persian army. Moreover, cognizant of the prior Persian defeats at Granicus and Issus, Darius had assembled directly opposite Alexander himself a crack force of Bactrian and Persian mailed cavalry, in addition to scythed chariots. Both Persian wings outflanked the Macedonians by more than a mile, and tough Greek mercenaries and elephants were prepared to crack Alexander's centre.

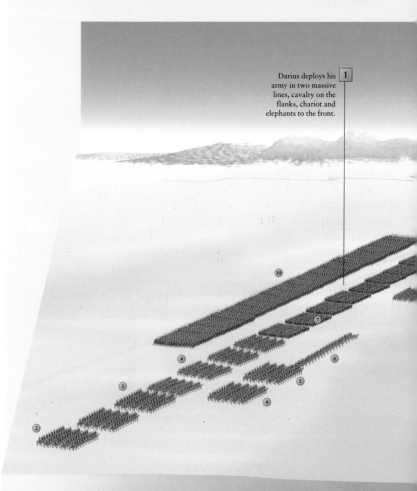

Darius deploys his **1** army in two massive lines, cavalry on the flanks, chariot and elephants to the front.

ALEXANDER THE GREAT (335–146)

DARIUS'S ARMY

1. Armenian cavalry
2. Cappadocian cavalry
3. Parthian cavalry
4. Median cavalry
5. Indian and Carion cavalry
6. Chariots
7. Persian infantry
8. Greek mercenaries
9. Bactrian and Persian cavalry
10. Infantry levies from many areas
11. Fifteen war elephants

ALEXANDER'S ARMY

1. Alexander and Companion cavalry
2. Macedonian archers
3. Agrianian javelin men
4. Hypaspiste
5. Macedonian phalanx
6. Thessalian cavalry
7. Cretan spearmen and archers
8. Left flank guard, cavalry
9. Right flank guard, cavalry, javalins and archers
10. Second line phalanx
11. Thracians

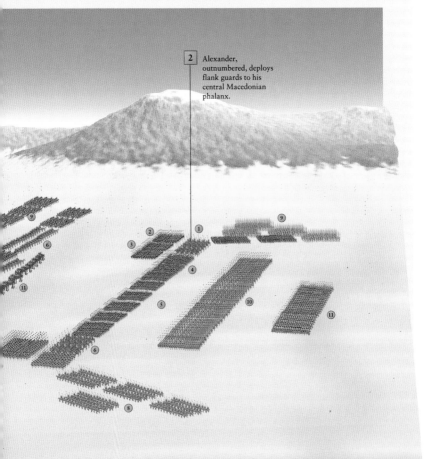

2 Alexander, outnumbered, deploys flank guards to his central Macedonian phalanx.

GAUGAMELA PHASE II

Darius planned to outflank both Alexander's wings and then crash through his weakened centre. In reality, the Macedonians bowed their line until the flanking Persians were over-extended and could be sliced through at their thinnest points. The key for the Macedonian left wing was to hold until Alexander broke through on the right.

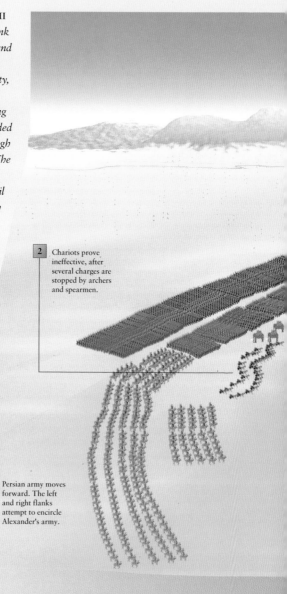

2 Chariots prove ineffective, after several charges are stopped by archers and spearmen.

1 Persian army moves forward. The left and right flanks attempt to encircle Alexander's army.

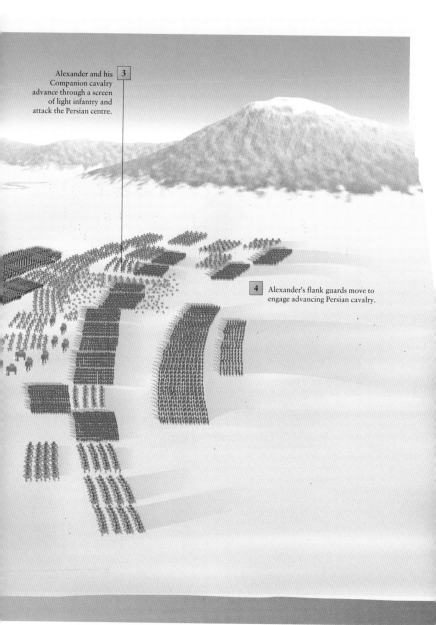

Alexander and his Companion cavalry advance through a screen of light infantry and attack the Persian centre. **3**

4 Alexander's flank guards move to engage advancing Persian cavalry.

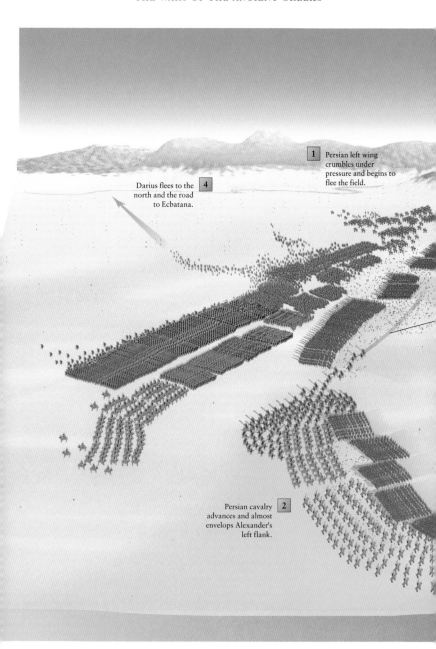

1 Persian left wing crumbles under pressure and begins to flee the field.

4 Darius flees to the north and the road to Ecbatana.

2 Persian cavalry advances and almost envelops Alexander's left flank.

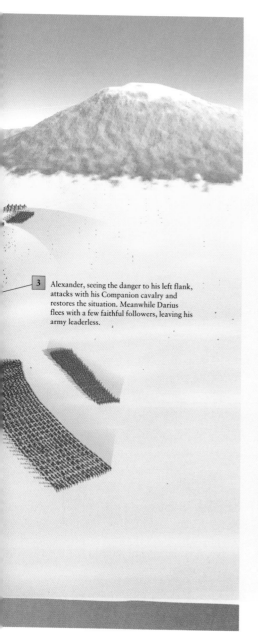

3 Alexander, seeing the danger to his left flank, attacks with his Companion cavalry and restores the situation. Meanwhile Darius flees with a few faithful followers, leaving his army leaderless.

GAUGAMELA PHASE III

The battle was won at three critical points. First, Alexander broke through a gap in the Persian left centre moments before he was outflanked. Second, Parmenio, vastly outnumbered on the left, held firm and prevented the Persians from getting behind the Macedonian line. Third, Darius fled before his army was defeated – his head-start at flight saving his life, but dooming those Persians still fighting gallantly on the battlefield. At day's end over 50,000 Persians were dead at a cost of a few hundred Macedonians.

defence, but our ancient sources more or less agree that on the city's final day of existence nearly 7,000 to 8,000 residents were butchered in the streets. Two thousand surviving males were then crucified as a lesson of the futility of resistance to Alexander the Great and his quest for a Brotherhood of Man. Perhaps anywhere from 20,000 to 30,000 women and children were enslaved. Tyre, like Thebes before, thus ceased to exist as a community.

Gaza, further south on the Syrian coast, was next. After a two-month siege Alexander let his troops murder the city's inhabitants at will. All males were exterminated, possibly between 10,000 Persians and Arabs died; every captured woman and child, numbering in the untold thousands, was sold into slavery. Alexander bound Batis, the governor of Gaza, pierced his ankles with thongs, and then dragged him around the city, Achilles-style, until the tortured victim expired.

But pitched battles and month-long sieges are merely the more dramatic events that capture the imagination of historians eager to appreciate the destructiveness of the Macedonian phalanx and siege apparatus, or to honour the personal leadership of Alexander on the battlefield. For most of the decade, Alexander fought in obscurity in the East, systematically burning villages, murdering local élites, and razing strongholds – rape is remarked on in our sources, as captive women were routinely handed over for the pleasure of the phalangites. Between the four dramatic pitched battles against the Persians and Indians, and the storming of dozens of cities and military garrisons, Alexander waged a relentless and mostly forgotten dirty war of attrition against the nomadic and tribal peoples of what is now modern-day Afghanistan, Iran and the Punjab. The list of devastated peoples is nearly endless, but a small sampling can give some idea of the sheer number of tribes that were either pacified or annihilated.

To the south of Susa the mountain villages of the Uxii of the Zagros mountains were systematically sacked and looted, and inhabitants killed or displaced (331). At the so-called Susian Gates, in western Iran, Alexander slaughtered the entire force of the satrap Ariobarzanes (331)

– only a handful of survivors escaped down the mountain. It took Alexander only five days to hunt down and conquer the Mardi of eastern Iran, who were now incorporated into Alexander's empire and forced to provide men, horses and hostages (331).

In Bactria, Alexander began to execute in earnest when faced with local revolts and succession. An expatriate community of Greeks, the so-called Branchideae, were wiped out to a man. Then it was the turn of the Sacai of Sogdiana, whose forces were extinguished and whose territory ravaged. Convinced that the rich villages of the Zervashan valley to the south had aided the rebellions in Sogdiana, Alexander stormed their fortresses and executed all the defenders he found (329) – 8,000 alone were killed in the capture of Cyrupolis. The revolts in Bactria and Sogdiana (329–328) were little more than two years of uninterrupted fighting, looting and executing.

Yet with Alexander's approach into India (327–326) the real barbarity begins. He massacred all the defenders along the river Choes in Bajaur. After promising the surrounded Assaceni their lives upon capitulation, he executed all their hired soldiers who surrendered; their other strongholds at Ora and Aornus were likewise stormed, and we should imagine that the garrisons were slaughtered also. The best example of Alexander's policy toward autonomous tribes and villagers in his path is that of the Malli of the lower Punjab. Most of their villages were razed and their civilian refugees butchered in the flight into the desert, prompting even Alexander's apologist, Sir William Tarn, to confess the campaign's 'dreadful record of mere slaughter'.

On his passage through the Gedrosian desert in 325, when his own men were not dying, Alexander destroyed the Oreitae. Arrian casually remarks that Alexander's lieutenant, Leonnatus, killed 6,000 of them in one engagement, and between famine and military conquest the Oreitae had their territory depopulated. Any estimation of the exact human costs of the subjugation of Bactria, Iran and India is impossible to make, but we should keep in mind that many of these villages and provincial strongholds were the homes of thousands, and after the arrival of Alexander most of their communities were destroyed and their male defenders either killed, enslaved, or recruited. So much for Tarn's idea that 'Alexander inspired Zeno's vision of a world in which all men should be ... citizens of one State without distinction of race or institutions, subject only to and in harmony with the Common Law immanent in the Universe, and united in one social life not by compulsion but only by their own willing consent or by Love.' The four-century evolution of Greek warfare had now come down to the mastery of murder on a grand scale.

On many occasions, Alexander's sheer recklessness and megalomania had disastrous consequences, when the expertise and advice of his generals and logisticians were ignored and the absence of postwar investigation assured. Two examples stand out: the sacking and conflagration of Persepolis and the ill-starred crossing of the Gedrosian desert. After the Persian capital was handed over in submission to Alexander, he allowed his Macedonians an entire day of plunder and killing. The historian Diodorus says they slaughtered anyone they met, pillaged the houses even of the common people, carried off the women, and sold into slavery any who survived the day of gratuitous killing. Plutarch, however, remarks that 'there was much slaughter of the prisoners who were taken'. And Curtius adds that many city residents preferred either to jump off the walls with their wives and children or to

On this enlarged close-up from a mosaic of the Roman period, which may well have been based on accurate paintings from the Hellenistic era, we receive the only real colour rendition of the young Alexander. Unlike most statues and coin portraiture, the artist has given a more realistic than idealistic Alexander, whose wide eyes, prominent nose, sideburns and unkempt stringy hair perhaps give a true picture of the young king in battle.

set fire to their households and families rather than be gutted in the streets. After a respite of a few months, all the imperial treasury was carted off – no precious metals were ever found in Persepolis by modern excavators – and the enormous palace torched amid a mass orgy of drunken debauchery. Fires probably spread beyond the palace and for a time left the capital uninhabitable. Documentary sources chronicle the immense loot gathered – 120,000 talents by most accounts, the material bounty requiring 10,000 pairs of mules and 5,000 camels to carry it away – but do not mention precise figures of the human cost. If Persepolis was capital of an empire of several million, and its population in the hundreds of thousands, we should imagine once again deaths in the thousands during the initial killing, subsequent enslavement, and final deportations and dispersals.

The rejection of the entire Hellenic tradition of civilian audit of the military now brought dire consequences even to Macedonian phalangites themselves, who would pay for Alexander's often poorly planned and maniac projects. Here one thinks immediately of his ill-fated idea of crossing the Gedrosian desert, his trek in the late summer of 325 along the northern coast of the Indian Ocean from the Indus river delta to the Persian Gulf. All ancient sources give lurid accounts of the suffering and death on the march of some 460 miles in sixty days. Alexander embarked with an army of at least 30,000 combatants, followed by a lengthy train of thousands more women and children. Arrian, Diodorus, Plutarch and Strabo speak of frightful losses to thirst, exhaustion and sickness, with tens of thousands left dead. Even if modern scholars are gullible in citing casualties of between 50,000 and 100,000 dead, it is nevertheless clear that in three months Alexander caused more deaths among his own troops than in a decade of losses to Persian soldiers. The real threat to the phalangites was not Darius, but their own crazed general.

Why march across a desert? There were other corridors of safer passage between Iran and India. Only a token force was needed to hike along the route to secure supply depots for Nearchus and his fleet which was cruising off the coast. The only plausible explanation for leading a huge army through such inhospitable lands was the sheer challenge that it offered to Alexander. There is ancient support for the idea that he sacrificed thousands of his own men in the pursuit of personal glory and adventure. His admiral Nearchus wrote that Alexander was keen to match the legendary feat of Semiramis, the Babylonian queen, and Cyrus the Great, who had both led armies through the wasteland. While the bulk of his infantry may have survived the ordeal, it is clear that thousands of camp followers died in the sand. In addition, every indigenous tribe in Alexander's path was subdued by force, their territory ravaged and plundered, leaving them in even worse straits than the invading army itself.

Finally, there is the matter of the executions, which were integral to Alexander's method of running his military. Unlike the practice of the city states, there were no shared commands by a board of generals, no civilian audits, no ostracism or court trials to oversee the Macedonian army. Alexander reacted to even suspicions of disloyalty with instant sentences of death, and it is no exaggeration that an entire generation of Macedonian noblemen was destroyed by the alcoholic king it served, the murders increasing with the paranoia and dementia of his final years. What is so striking about his execution of friends and associates is the long record of personal loyalty and service the condemned gave to the young king. Besides the well-known murdered Macedonian grandees, there is a host of lesser-known bureaucrats who were summarily killed on unproven charges of disloyalty, incompetence or intrigue. More repugnant still is Alexander's sometimes personal intervention in the torture and execution of his adversaries, occasions where his genius was directed to novel manners of torture. Generalship in the Greek world was now a long way from civic leaders like Pericles and Epaminondas; instead it had evolved into a bizarre and deadly mixture of political autocracy, pop mysticism, and sadistic megalomania.

Philip II, Alexander's father, may well have been assassinated by a cabal, perhaps involving Olympias and Alexander himself, the discarded wife and half-Macedonian son, who were to be nonentities among the dozens of wives (seven at the king's death), concubines, legitimate and illegitimate sons that would result during the expected long reign of Philip. Upon succession, Alexander had murdered the two brothers, Arrhabaeus and Heromenes, the sons of the Macedonian noble Aeropus, at his father's funeral, along with a few other high-ranking and thus suspicious élites. Then almost every prominent Macedonian who was not immediately aligned with Alexander was murdered – Amyntas, son of Perdiccas, the general Attalus and his relatives, Philip's last wife Cleopatra and her infant, Alexander's half-sister. While in Asia, he had Alexander Lyncestis executed, his first supporter in his struggle for regal succession.

The mock trial and subsequent torture and stoning of his general Philotas (330) are well known. Far from being a conspirator, Philotas, who had shared co-command of the Macedonian cavalry and had fought heroically in all Alexander's major campaigns, was guilty of little more than arrogance and failure to pass on gossip about possible dissension against the king. Unfortunately, he was loyal to his father Parmenio, the famous old general who anchored the Macedonian left wing, and whose bravery had saved Alexander on more than one occasion. Thus with Philotas's gruesome death, the veteran Parmenio – no charges were ever brought – was murdered as well, his head sent to Alexander as proof that the bastion of the old-guard Macedonian élite, who had created his army and ensured his succession, was now gone. By the time he was 70, Parmenio had lost all his sons in Alexander's grand enterprise – Nicanor and Hector in campaigning, Philotas now tortured and stoned – and the price he finally paid for his loyalty to Alexander was his own decapitation.

Various other Macedonian nobles either disappeared or were killed outright as the army moved further east. Cleitus, the so-called 'Black Cleitus', who had saved Alexander at the Granicus, was speared to death by the intoxicated king himself at a drunken banquet. After a number of young Macedonian pages were stoned to death for suspicion of sedition (327), Alexander executed the philosopher Callisthenes, nephew of Aristotle, who had objected to the king's practice of *proskynesis*, or having all kneel before him in eastern fashion. And after emerging from the Gedrosian desert, Alexander went on a seven-day binge of drink and revelry which culminated in a series of further execution decrees. The generals Cleander and Sitacles – and perhaps later Agathon and Heracon – and 600 of their troops were killed without warning or legal trial, purportedly on charges of either malfeasance or insubordination, but more likely because of their involvement in carrying out Alexander's order to execute the popular Parmenio – a move that had not gone down well with the rank-and-file veterans and now required some ceremonial show of expiation. Thus without evidence or trial, Alexander decimated an entire corps of 6,000 men – the first clear evidence of the practice in western warfare, but one that must have made a notable impression on the Romans.

Alexander the Great's legacy was to leave the Hellenistic world with generations of would-be Alexanders, who practised their master's savage brand of political autocracy and butchery of all under suspicion. The army in the West was now not to be a militia or even a professional force subject to civilian oversight, but, like the later Nazi military, an autocratic tool that would murder at will far from the battlefield, friend and foe, soldier and civilian alike. Alexander the Great was no philosopher–king, not even a serious colonizer or administrator, and surely not a well-meaning emissary of Hellenism. Instead, he was an energetic, savvy adolescent, who inherited from his father a frighteningly murderous army and the loyal cadre of very shrewd and experienced battle administrators who knew how to take such a lethal show on the road.

Classically educated, and endowed with natural brilliance and little fear, Alexander had a keen appreciation of ceremony and the role of personal magnetism on the battlefield amid thousands of volatile paid killers eager solely for booty and adventure in a decade-long spree of

bloodshed and spoliation. Were it not for his tactical brilliance, Alexander the Great's career is what we might expect of a reckless and selfish man in his twenties, who could drink, travel, kill, and fight when and where he wished until his body gave out and his

The climactic moments of the battle of Issus (333) are captured in this famous Roman floor mosaic from Pompeii, from which the earlier portrait of Alexander was taken. Darius III amidst his bodyguard catches the deadly gaze of the charging Alexander who is intent on his destruction. Notice the wall of Macedonian sarissas to the rear of the Persian king, which suggests the imminent breakthrough of Alexander's phalangites. Ancient accounts claim that Darius was one of the first to flee from the battlefield.

terrorized subordinates, after marching over 15,000 miles at his bequest, could at last take no more.

The Hellenistic age began with Alexander's final destruction of Greek freedom and political autonomy. His introduction of Greek military culture beyond the Aegean and the economic stimulus of flooding the Greek world with the stored and previously untapped gold and silver of the imperial Persian treasuries fuelled a nightmare of political oppression and widening economic inequality, of exploiting monarchies in place of autonomous polities. Councils, middling hoplites and a free voting citizenry were never to return, as Alexander's Hellenism meant élite kings, autocrats and landless peasants – all backed by ferocious hired thugs. Militiamen gave way to paid mercenaries, and war consumed capital and manpower at rates unimaginable just a few decades earlier. The old idea of the man of politics being separate from the religious leader was now lost, as the notion of an eastern divinity on the throne became the norm – with all the accustomed megalomania, gratuitous slaughter and oppression that we associate with theocratic states. Religion was now to be integral to warfare as armies were mobilized on the pretext of divine guidance. If anything, Alexander diluted and then undermined the best of what Hellenism had promised for politics and religion – and ended for good the Greek idea that free men away from the battlefield determine when and where to fight. But these assessments are mere disagreements over taste and values. In the last analysis military historians must find common ground among the dead.

Too many scholars like to compare Alexander to Hannibal or Napoleon. A far better match would be Hitler, who engineered a militarily brilliant but similarly brutal killing march into Russia during the summer and autumn of 1941. Both Alexander and Hitler were crack-pot mystics, intent solely on loot and plunder under the guise of bringing 'culture' to the East and 'freeing' oppressed peoples from a corrupt empire. Both were kind to animals, showed deference to women, talked constantly of their own destiny and divinity, and could be especially courteous to subordinates even as they planned the destruction of hundreds of thousands, and murdered their closest associates.

In sum, Alexander's decade-long expedition to the Indus resulted in death and displacement for millions, and the enslavement of thousands more, earning him rightly a place amid the worst monsters history has to offer. Western warfare was now to be total: killing men in the field, on the run, in their homes, families and all – killing even one's own lieutenants if need be, killing relatives, friends, anyone at any time at all. In the end, the legacy of this drunken brawler is one of murder, ethnic cleansing and genocide, and we would do well to remember his dead – always the dead. Under thirteen years of generalship of Alexander the Great, more people were killed through his use of western warfare than had died in all the Greek battles in the century and a half from Marathon to Chaeronea. And his successors were eager to continue.

THE SUCCESSORS, THE COMING OF ROME AND THE COLLAPSE OF GREEK WARFARE

Upon Alexander's death in 323 the remains of the Persian empire were divided among his successors, the senior Macedonian commanders in the field and those back at home in Greece – most of whom were happy to see the unbalanced and murderous youth gone. The old-guard generals Perdiccas, Craterus and Eumenes were quickly eliminated, and spheres of influence tentatively allotted to the other surviving underlings: Antipater controlled Macedonia and Greece; Ptolemy received Egypt; Antigonus occupied Asia Minor; Seleucus inherited Mesopotamia and the East as far as India; Lysimachus retained Thrace and territory around the Black Sea. Seleucus' subsequent victory at Ipsus in 301 over the 81-year-old Antigonus the One Eyed and his son Demetrius proved that no one general was to inherit Alexander's legacy. And so, for the next century and a half, rival Macedonian dynasts fought a series of inconclusive wars throughout the Greek and Asiatic world, in futile attempts to reconstitute Alexander's brief kingdom, hiring and stealing from a pool of nearly 100,000 Greek mercenaries in the east who had seen service at some time with Alexander or his lieutenants.

By the end of the fourth century it was not so much the demand for hired killers as the enormous reservoir of the unemployed that accounts for the mercenary explosion. The blinkered *polis* idea of equating agricultural ownership and production exclusively with citizenship and military service was inflexible in the face of enormous cultural and economic transformations in the Mediterranean unleashed by the succession of Athenian imperialism, the rise of Macedon and the fall of Persia. A growing number of hungry Greek 'outsiders' now cared little whether they had a seat in the assembly hall or were esteemed militiamen in the phalanx of some parochial state.

For the military historian the battles of the so-called Successors reveal an undeniable fascination: pikes lengthen to more than 20 feet, elephants make routine appearances, enormous and garish siege-engines assault cities. Indeed, the emptied treasuries, capital and displaced manpower that flowed from the disruption of Persian hegemony made a Hellenistic weapons race inevitable. Once unlimited coinage was devoted to warmaking, and the technical and philosophical genius of the Greeks was applied to the new military science, organized killing became a Greek art form in itself.

We can note the hallmarks of Hellenistic warfare in a variety of areas. The sheer magnitude of warmaking is perhaps the most remarkable. Antigonus may have invaded Egypt (306) with nearly 100,000 men, the largest Greek-speaking army since the Panhellenic muster at Plataea over 170 years earlier. At Ipsus (301), there may have been nearly a quarter of a million men arrayed against each other in the respective armies of Antigonus and Seleucus, and perhaps 500 elephants. At later battles such at Raphia (217), and Pyrrhus' battles of Heraclea (280) and Asculum (279) against the Romans, the respective Greek forces probably fielded well over 50,000 infantry, cavalry and light-armed troops. Armies no longer marched for three days, but criss-crossed thousands of miles of Alexander's former empire, requiring enormous fleets to transport them across the Adriatic, Aegean and Mediterranean.

Size meant cost. To pay for such armies, Hellenistic generals relied on booty, and here too figures for plunder are staggering. Alexander enslaved and sold 30,000 citizens after the destruction of Thebes in 335, and 20,000 after the battle at the Granicus in 334. He carted off 125,000 talents after putting the Persian capital of Persepolis to the torch – or roughly the monetary equivalent of more than 750 million man-days of mercenary service, money to keep a mercenary army of 50,000 in the field every day for forty consecutive years. That figure was in addition to the almost 50,000 talents he had already robbed from the Persian regional treasury at Susa in the same year. In 307 after his victory over Ptolemy off Cyprus, Demetrius captured 8,000 soldiers, 100 supply ships, and 40 warships complete with their crews.

Military construction reflected the vast sums involved. At the siege of Rhodes in 305–304 Demetrius had built an absurd *helepolis* or 'city-taker', a mobile, armoured tower 140 feet in height and weighing 150 tons. This monstrosity housed over 200 combatants, and required over 3,000 labourers to move, yet was only to be withdrawn from the siege when the Rhodians knocked off several of its iron plates, making it vulnerable to fire. In one night alone, Rhodian artillery fired 800 fire-bolts and 1,500 catapult bolts at the *helepolis*. A single bolt worth no more than a drachma might disable a machine worth hundreds of thousands. The 'city-taker's' construction, maintenance – and loss – consumed the capital of thousands of days of man labour. And for nothing – Rhodes withstood the siege anyway. This was impractical gigantism on a magnitude comparable to the contemporary B-2 American bomber, whose two billion dollar price tag precludes its use in most military operations – it too can be brought down by a cheap missile worth far less than the plane's windshield.

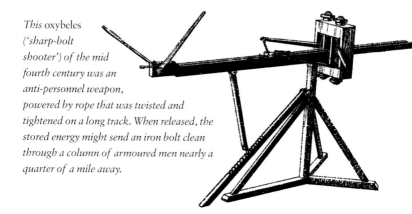

This oxybeles ('sharp-bolt shooter') of the mid fourth century was an anti-personnel weapon, powered by rope that was twisted and tightened on a long track. When released, the stored energy might send an iron bolt clean through a column of armoured men nearly a quarter of a mile away.

In this age of senseless construction, ships dwarfed the old trireme that had been manned by 170 oarsmen and another 30 assorted marines, archers and deck-hands. Now *hepteres* (seven men to an oar) might reach 140 feet in length, need crews of 350 rowers, 200 marines, and be outfitted with a massive bronze ram and catapults. Ptolemy IV purportedly constructed an enormous top-heavy ship of 4,000 oarsmen and 3,200 infantry, 40 men stationed at each oar. Such battleships might cost ten times more to construct and man than the agile and swift Classical trireme, as battle was to be fought in or near harbours between fewer and larger ships. These boats served more as platforms for infantry than as naval assets, and lacked the skilled oarage and sleek design necessary for sophisticated ramming tactics.

Fortifications were also now far larger, with towers more frequent and taller with more apertures for artillery. They were also surrounded by ditches and field walls, and palisaded to disrupt the clear passage of offensive siege engines. Expensive technology was even applied to the mundane, as for example when Cleomenes' troops invaded Argos in 222 equipped with special wood shafts that had been crafted expressly to destroy grain – even agricultural devastation was to be improved with technology.

But not all costs were material. More men now died than ever before in pitched battle. The Greeks had lost less than a thousand at Marathon and Plataea combined, and even during the great hoplite disasters of the Classical *polis* – Delium (424) and Leuctra (371) – the total Greek dead was less than 3,000. But now soldiers were butchered in their thousands in a matter of hours, due to longer pikes, less body armour, the greater use of missile troops, cavalry and elephants, the recklessness in the use of hired professionals, and the sheer size of mercenary armies. At the most extreme, perhaps 20,000 were killed at Ipsus (301). Yet even at smaller engagements like Raphia (217) between Ptolemy and Antiochus almost 15,000 fell. And when phalanx met legion, the use of the Roman *gladius*, or short sword, ensured even more dead – nearly 30,000 phalangites and legionaries fell at Heraclea in 280. There were as many as 9,000 combined Greek and Roman fatalities at Cynoscephalae in 197, and perhaps 20,000 or more at Pydna in 168.

In general, there was a clear trend of growing battle mortality from the seventh to the second century: Classical hoplite battles resulted in perhaps 10 to 20 per cent of the combined forces on the battlefield killed; Hellenistic 30 to 40 per cent; and in legionary engagements, perhaps 50 to 80 per cent of those assembled – albeit the great majority of the latter non-Roman – might die in a single day. Indeed, the killing that went on in Hellenistic and Roman battles was limited solely by inanimate laws of physics – the degree of savagery that muscular powered iron might accomplish against flesh in a set time and space.

Where did the men and money come from to fuel the insanity? In general, two explanations account for the enormous Hellenistic investment in military technology and the greater size of armies and navies. First, the sheer scale of robbery of old Persian treasuries at Sardis, Ecbatana, Susa, Babylon and Persepolis tapped tons of uncoined gold and silver that for decades had been accumulated – and hoarded – from the tribute of Persian imperial subjects. The release of these precious metals in the form of regional coinages of the

Successors meant a general inflation of the Mediterranean economy for the next two centuries. And along with money came a much larger pool of new mercenary recruits from Asia, Persia, Media, Bactria, India and Africa, easterners previously outside the orbit of western warfare, who were now eager for regular pay and the plunder and booty that were often the wages of Hellenistic battle.

Second, the general introduction of property and income taxes and forced contributions to pay for professional war spelled the end of the old agrarian councils of the Greek city state. Inscriptions may record civic legislation of Hellenistic Greek cities, but such standardized decrees mirrored more the obsequious behaviour of the apparat in modern collective societies than the rough and tumble activity of true consensual and tight-fisted local governments.

This gradual withdrawal of yeomen from the Greek countryside and active political life also had two reciprocal and profound effects on the warmaking of the times. First, wars could now be longer and year-round, as armies were largely composed of wage-earners who sought regular pay, rather than farmers whose back-breaking work often meant handing over harvest recompense to urban grandees. Almost all records of public loans on stone catalogued from the fourth century and later reveal the necessity of defence – reflecting the extraordinary degree to which Greek culture had become militarized. Second, the continual enslavement of captured peoples and the subsequent greater use of slaves in both agriculture and manufacturing by well-connected élites meant a growing urbanism. Cities like Alexandria, Pergamon or Syracuse were far larger than even the grandest Classical *poleis*. Thus there was a rich pool of itinerant craftsmen, mercenaries and skilled workers who were less concerned with civic government and costly public subsidies for theatre attendance, participation in the assembly, or service on juries. Instead, royal regimes attracted talent for military construction and service and left the bothersome business of politics to their own courts. Available capital for war then increased in both relative and absolute ways: less money was needed for the participation of fewer citizens in municipal government and culture – and more was gained by allowing innovative and ruthless men to mount invasions that were little more than organized robberies.

Within this period during the third and second centuries, two notable Greek military theatres emerged in the Mediterranean: the invasion into Italy of the Greek king Pyrrhus (280–275), and the Roman campaigns on the Greek mainland and in Asia Minor (Cynoscephalae in 197, Magnesia in 189, Pydna in 168) against a succession of Macedonian and Greek armies under Philip V, Antiochus III, and Philip's son Perseus. Out of these battle victories over the Hellenistic Greeks and Macedonians appears the clear superiority of a new military formation, the legion, and with it the coming of Rome.

The latter had learned a great deal from both the Classical and the Hellenistic Greeks, avoiding the parochialism of the former and the extravagant corruption of the latter. Thus the legion had superseded the old Roman phalanx, combining ideas of decisive shock battle together with the advantages of missiles and skirmishing: the legionary might throw his javelin, then advance either in mass with locked shields or in waves of independent corps, as infantrymen carved out a path with their swords. Hellenic warfare had never mastered the proper balance between aerial and hand attack – a unity that the Romans now brought to the individual legionary himself, who could kill his opponent equally well from inches or from yards away.

Yeomen of a unified and republican Italy provided the necessary manpower, as a professional centurion class moulded naturally spirited agrarians into trained swordsmen and ordered marchers. In some sense, the Republican militias, with their emphasis on group solidarity, patriotism, and belief in a superior culture, were more Greek than the Hellenistic military dynasties they met: the armies of Alexander's *epigonoi* had become every bit as despotic, top heavy and corrupt as the old Persian imperial levies, whom the Greeks had conquered almost two centuries earlier.

True, nothing could ever match the sheer terror of a Macedonian-style phalanx – the historian Curtius said that phalangites were 'tough, tightly packed soldiers who cannot be budged'. The Roman general Aemilius Paulus, who faced phalangites at Pydna, was left with a lifelong image of terror: 'He considered the formidable appearance of their front, bristling with arms, and was taken with fear and alarm: nothing he had ever seen before was its equal. Much later he frequently used to recall that sight and his own reaction to it.' Nor could any enemy neglect the wide arsenal – heavy and light cavalry, light infantry, skirmishers, slingers, bowmen and elephants –

Other than in coin portraiture and individual statues, almost all commemorative art after Alexander's death captures the king in battle, as on this marble sarcophagus that was commissioned shortly after his death. Alexander's sarcophagus is now displayed in the Turkish National Museum in Istanbul.

that megalomaniac Hellenistic commanders might theoretically bring on to the battlefield.

Nevertheless, after Alexander there were inherent weaknesses in Hellenistic military practice on both a tactical and a strategic level. By the third century, almost all phalangites were exclusively hired mercenaries. Gone was any vestigial sense of national solidarity and professional *élan* of the old Macedonian companions. But unlike the lean forces of Philip and Alexander of even a few decades before, these much larger hired forces of the Successors required enormous non-combatant support: baggage carriers, engineers, wives, children, slaves and markets. Such logistical and social dependence was often only haphazard and inefficiently organized. This relative sloppiness limited the strategic options of a Hellenistic army, as the occupation and control of conquered ground was increasingly a question only of cash, not of national interest, courage, or the patriotism of local citizenry.

More important, the phalanx itself had grown unwieldy when heavy pikes approached 20 or more feet in length – an armchair tactician's fascinating nightmare. But the tradition of cavalry symphony under Alexander was neglected at just the period when cumbersome Macedonian infantry needed even greater integration, its flanks more, not less, protection by horsemen. This infatuation with gigantism was more a reflection of imperial prestige and dynastic rivalry than a response to military challenge. Elephants – fixtures of ancient warfare from Gaugamela (331) to Thapsus (46) – and local mercenary cavalry were not the answer, as the successor generals simplistically tried to match the lost tactical skill of Alexander with purchased manpower and brute force of arms. Gone were the haughty companion cavalry, masterful horsemen and estate owners who felt themselves the equals of the king himself. Increased power without grace simply made the phalanx more vulnerable than ever.

Vulnerable, but not without terror. The historian Livy remarked that each Roman legionary was targeted by ten pikes of the phalanx, the 'demand' of the crowded spearheads was greater than the 'supply' of available enemy targets. Each Macedonian pikeman sought to maintain his weapon horizontally, jabbing back and forth to occupy critical empty space should a legionary try to find a wedge between the tips. But if a row of pikes went down from a sea of thrown Roman *pila*, if enemy Roman swordsmen were catapulted into the interior, or, worse, crashed in from the naked sides of the phalanx, disaster was immediate. The secondary dagger – as ridiculously small as the pike was absurdly big – offered little protection for the Macedonian and was a sorry match for the Roman *gladius*, the double-edged sword of Spanish steel. In addition the pike itself was impossible to wield against the immediate infiltrator facing the pikeman. But for the phalangite to throw the spear down, to high-tail it unheroically to the rear – that would only open the breach even wider, and ignominious flight was largely futile anyway, given the compression of bodies.

Once inside the columns enemy legionaries carved at the bellies, groins and limbs of stunned and trapped phalangites with abandon, until the entire mass of the phalanx simply disintegrated, men frozen, trying to hold their pikes firm as they were in fact disemboweled. Livy remarks that Greeks had never seen the type of carnage – severed limbs and torsos – that Roman swordplay might inflict.

At Cynoscephalae (197) rough terrain and the flexibility of the Roman foot soldiers halted Macedonian momentum, and the legions killed thousands of Philip V's men. And at Pydna two decades later, Philip's son Perseus had no better luck, as legionaries once again found gaps in the phalanx and cut the interior to shreds – more than 20,000 phalangites were butchered. The Romans had sensed how Hellenistic weakness involved more than just the clumsiness of the phalanx, extending to the very infrastructure of government, manpower, generalship and finance. Without a notion of a federated Greek nation, a Hellenistic army's survival depended entirely on its reserves of cash and its own battlefield reputation to attract recruits – both could be destroyed by a single defeat.

The Hellenistic autocrats had found their phalanxes unconquerable against Asiatic troops, and adequate enough against one another. But Rome brought to each battle a haughty new bellicosity and bureaucracy of war – hospitals, doctors, rigid discipline, standardized weapons, trained soldiers, skilled officers – which were the material and spiritual dividends of a united and politically stable Italy. Moreover the machinery of Roman war was not brilliantly haphazard, but systematized, lessening the armies' vulnerability to occasional bad generalship, weather, or strategic folly. The legions were often led to their slaughter by bad generals, their magnetic leaders killed, without harming the blueprint that would clone identical forces from scratch. And unlike Hellenistic battle practice, Roman warfare was always presented as a legal necessity, a purportedly defensive undertaking that was forced by belligerents upon the rural folk of Italy. While their generals may have killed for *laus* and *gloria*, the republican legionaries themselves thought they fought to preserve the traditions of their ancestors and in accordance with the constitutional decrees of an elected government.

By 146 the last Hellenic resistance to Roman military authority ended with the destruction of Corinth and the end of the federated Achaean League. Western warfare, however, now entered a phase of nearly six centuries of military dominance. True, Roman armies continued to win because they added their own novel contributions of regularization to decisive war. But at its heart, Roman militarism was based on mass confrontation in pitched battles, and on applying the entire engine of Hellenic-inspired science, economic practice and political structure to exploit such battlefield aggressiveness in annihilating the enemy. The Greek way of warfare, then, was not really dead. For the next two millennia in Europe, battle would be energized as never before by those who were not Greeks. Soldiers in Europe would inherit the peculiarly western dilemma of the Greeks of having free rein to kill and conquer when they often knew they should not.

Conclusion: the Hellenic legacy

THE PHENOMENAL RECORD OF Greek military prowess is unquestioned. After Xerxes' failed invasion of 480, Greece remained free from foreign invasion until the Roman conquest three centuries later – and the triumphant legions of Rome owed much of their battle success to the hallowed Greek approach to warfare. No non-western invader after 480 could occupy and hold the Greek mainland for long until the Ottoman subjugation two thousand years later. And for nearly a half millennia before the Roman conquest (700–146), Greeks would sail up the Nile, colonize the Black Sea, the Aegean and parts of the Mediterranean, and conquer Persia. Hoplites and phalangites fought as mercenaries in Egypt, marched to the Indus and under Pyrrhus criss-crossed Italy and Sicily. Greek armour would spread to Illyria, Scythia and Persia and be copied by military designers from Italy to southern Russia. The Greek science of ballistics was responsible for the vast arsenal of Roman artillery, which slaughtered Britons and Jews alike 2,000 miles apart. The Byzantine army for a millennium (500–1500) would protect its beleaguered domain through the preservation of Greek military organization and science.

The tally of the Hellenic battlefield reflects the deadly nature of the Greeks' approach to warmaking. Thousands of Persians were slain at Marathon, Thermopylae, Salamis and Plataea against a few hundred Greeks. Alexander destroyed an empire of millions while losing less than a thousand phalangites in pitched battle; indeed, he killed more Greeks and Macedonians than did his Eastern enemies. More Greeks perished in the internecine Peloponnesian war than all those slain by Darius and Xerxes a half century earlier. When Carthaginians, Persians, Italians and Egyptians looked for military guidance there was usually a Greek willing to offer his society's martial expertise for a price. This was a culture, after all, in which Polybius remarked that successful generals, in addition to having experience, courage, practical sense and knowledge of tactics and strategy, should also master geometry and astronomy – a culture whose armies also made little distinction between élite and mass: a Spartan king at Thermopylae lost his head alongside his men; the founder of western philosophy was almost killed in his late forties at Delium; the greatest orator in the history of the *polis* took up his shield and spear at Chaeronea.

How are we to account for the uniquely lethal warmaking of these most extraordinary Greeks? How did a relatively isolated people of less than two million in the southern Balkans change the character of civilization in the ancient Mediterranean, in the process founding the principles of later western warfare itself? Location and climate alone do not suffice. True, Greece was hemmed in to the east by the vast empires of Persia and the dynastic Egyptians, Hittites and Assyrians. All had maritime access to Europe via the Aegean and Mediterranean. Tribes in eastern Europe and the northern Balkans were not more than a few weeks' march from the northern plains of Thessaly. Thus from earliest times the Greeks were forced to defend themselves from Thracians, Gauls and Persians – or perish. But many, far wealthier empires in their rough neighbourhood – the Mycenaeans, Egypt, Persia and Phoenicia – in fact, did perish much earlier than they. Bellicose enemies and ever-present dangers in themselves do not necessarily translate into excellence in arms.

Does the climate of the Mediterranean explain the Greek mastery of warfare? For centuries historians have explained the Greeks' revolutionary turn toward consensual government, public ceremony and civic art and drama as inseparable from a temperate climate that ensured for most of the year that the citizenry would neither freeze nor be scorched when outdoors, making possible amphitheatres, breezy porticoes, the agora and the open-air assembly hall. Similarly, did the absence of snow, jungles and vast deserts allow hoplite militias to muster easily each summer, assured of good campaigning weather, in which they could camp out, see their enemy and find accessible food, forage and water? After all, decisive battle between massed armies of heavy-armed infantrymen is difficult in the Sahara, the Amazon or in the ice of

Scandinavia. Yet the Greeks were beneficiaries of temperate weather only to the same degree as north Africans and other southern Europeans in Spain and France, whose militaries in comparison to the armies of Greece and Rome were unsophisticated. It is true, of course, that thinkers as diverse as Herodotus, Hippocrates, Plato and Xenophon felt that the rugged terrain of Greece and its temperate climate – short winters without tropical summers – created tough bodies and minds, which were not brutalized by a savage north or enervated by a lazy south. But even if one accepts such dubious geographical determinism, we are still left again with the incongruity that Greek military prowess is singular even within the Mediterranean belt from Spain to Phoenicia – and not duplicated in similar climates the world over.

All that is not to say that terrain and climate did not affect the nature of Greek land warfare, especially the rise of lethal infantry forces of the *polis*. The phalanx was a manifestation of a free citizenry, which fought in a manner that served to uphold the values of an autonomous yeomanry. But before we use the nomenclature of social science to characterize hoplite war as 'socially constructed' or 'ritualized', a type of artificial fighting intended to valorize a particular landowning class within the *polis*, we should also remember, as Plato reminds us in his *Laws*, that the manner of Hellenic fighting also mirrored the physical landscape of Greece itself. Flat plains such as those found in Thessaly and coastal Macedon favoured horse-raising and the culture of cavalry, while in more mountainous areas such as Aetolia, Acarnania and Crete – the ideal enclaves of herdsmen – skirmishing and missile attack were more the norm. In contrast, most of the major city states – Argos, Athens, Corinth, Mantinea, Sparta and Thebes – were situated amid valleys surrounded and divided by nearby mountain ranges. Such small, fertile and rolling plains not only favoured the culture of small farming, but also allowed heavy infantrymen to march unencumbered and provided little natural shelter for less armoured ambushers. The nearby hills also protected the flanks of such ponderous infantry columns from the sweeps of horsemen.

If one farmed on small plains surrounded by hills and wished to protect that ground, there was a logic to wearing such ostensibly impractical heavy armour and massing in column. Out of that physical and cultural matrix, then, arises the birth of western warfare – the primacy of heavily armoured free hoplites who would fight in the summer decisively on the farmland surrounding their autonomous communities. Greek warfare is a product of time and space in the sense that the climate and terrain of Greece and its relative initial isolation from the Eastern Mediterranean, permitted its strange culture of the *polis* to survive and flourish until it was mature enough to spread beyond mainland Greece.

That being said, two notable revolutions characterize Greek warfare – the birth of the city state in the eighth century BC and its decline in the fourth. Ideas and values, not location or weather, were what distinguished the Greeks. The rise of hoplite militias of the *polis* created the idea of western warfare as decisive infantry battle waged by free men over property and local autonomy – quite in contrast with both the spirit and purpose of war that had preceded it anywhere in the Mediterranean, which was often waged by peasants, serfs and mercenaries for booty, hegemony and royal succession. But unlike the catastrophic end to the Mycenaean Age and the subsequent four centuries of impoverishment of the Dark Ages, the Hellenistic World that followed the classical city state in the fourth century BC was in some sense a continuum – free inquiry, rationalism and capitalism continued, albeit without the consensual government, the chauvinism of a middling citizenry and autonomy of the *polis*. In a military context, after the fourth century, decisive battle, superior technology, rigid discipline, sophisticated logistics and organization of the *polis* were to be freed from parochialism and civilian audit, and thus western warfare evolved into a deadly business engaging the full arsenal of past Hellenic science and manpower. The rise of the *polis* created the idea of decisive battle between doughty infantrymen; its decline freed that concept from ethical constraint. Regardless of the personal preferences of the combatants involved, the free Greeks who died at Chaeronea in 338 had voted to fight there; the deadlier phalangites in the army of Philip who killed them had not.

That dual legacy of the Greeks was to inspire most of later European warmaking during the medieval period and Renaissance, as military planners sought to preserve the idea of civic militarism of the Greeks within the general Hellenistic landscape of superior technology and tactics. Vegetius was translated into the modern European languages to glean information on how to organize and equip armies. Phalanxes themselves were to reappear in Switzerland, Germany and Italy, as Renaissance abstract thinkers sought to apply ancient discussions of *stratêgia* (generalship) and *taktika* (the arrangement of troops) to improving the crash of contemporary pikemen. Pragmatists as diverse as Machiavelli, Lipsius and Grotius also sought to employ such armies in constitutional service to the state, realizing that heavy infantrymen, mustered from free yeoman citizens, were the most effective troops when engaged in mass collision. And by the Enlightenment the old Hellenic idea of rules and protocols was to reappear as efforts to curb warmaking, or at least to employ it in defensive purposes, in line with either Christian teaching or the growing ideals of rational humanism.

The twentieth century, of course, changed that traditional western notion of the need to muster citizen armies for just wars fought to preserve family, home and culture. The Classical idea that a long peace at any cost created decadence, effeminacy and a commercial rather than a spiritual citizenry – best phrased by Polybius, Sallust, Livy and Juvenal, but also reiterated by Kant and Hegel – could not survive the ghastly reality of the Somme and Verdun. Indeed, between Classical antiquity and the present age lie the trenches of the First World War, the carpet bombing of the Second World War, the death camps and the apocalyptic threat of the Third World War. Thus intellectuals in general have been quick to point out the senselessness of trench warfare, the needless destruction of Dresden or the sheer absurdity of Mutually

Assured Destruction. Rarely have they couched that reproach in the Hellenic spirit of criticizing unwise tactics and unnecessary strategies within the parameters of a very necessary conflict against Prussian militarism, Axis fascism and Soviet totalitarianism. We have lost faith, partly due to our technology, partly as a result of our recent history, in the Greeks' clear-cut notion of good and evil and the necessity of free people to fight frequently to preserve their liberty.

So modern western man finds himself in a dilemma. His excellence at frontal assault and decisive battle – now expanded to theatres both above the earth's atmosphere and below the sea – might end all that he holds dear despite the nobility of his cause and the moral nature of his warmaking. We in the West may well have to fight as non-westerners – in jungles, stealthily at night and as counter-terrorists – to combat enemies who dare not face us in battle. In consequence, we cannot fully draw on our great Hellenic traditions of superior technology and the discipline and ardour of our free citizen soldiers.

I leave the reader with the paradox that in the modern age, the western manner of fighting bequeathed to us from the Greeks is so destructive and so lethal that we have essentially reached an impasse. Few non-westerners wish to meet our armies in battle – the only successful response to encountering a western army is to marshal another western army. But the state of technology and escalation is now such that any inter-western conflict would have the opposite result of its original Hellenic intent – abject slaughter on both sides would result, rather than quick resolution. Whereas the *polis* Greeks discovered shock battle as a glorious method of saving lives and confining conflict to an hour's worth of heroics between armoured infantry, their successors in the Hellenistic and Roman worlds sought to unleash the entire power of their culture to destroy one another in a horrendous moment – and twentieth-century man has at last realized just that moment.

Glossary

AGRARIAN. The Greek ideal of the early city state whereby the countryside should be divided up into small, equally sized parcels, whose ownership provided the citizen with political rights in the Assembly and a responsibility to fight as a hoplite in the phalanx.

ARCHAIC. The two-century period from the establishment of the city state (700) to the end of the Persian wars (479), when war was largely defined as battle between phalanxes of heavy hoplite infantry.

ATTICA. The rural hinterlands around Athens, whose region and population, together with Athens proper, formed the Athenian state.

BASILEIS. Literally Greek for 'kings', but in the Homeric context used of élite warriors.

BOEOTIA. A rich agricultural territory in central Greece; by the fourth century federated under the democratic leadership of its chief city, Thebes. Sometimes in a fourth-century context Boeotia is used almost indistinguishably from Thebes itself.

CLASSICAL. Chronological period that begins after the Persian wars (479) and extends to the end of the free autonomous city state at Chaeronea (338), characterized by an increasing variety of military forces and theatres as hoplite militias were augmented by mercenaries and non-infantry forces.

DARK AGES. A loosely defined era between the fall of the Mycenaean citadels and the rise of the city state (1200–800), when sophisticated civilization vanished, population declined, and material culture was largely impoverished.

HELLENISTIC. Generally recognized period from the death of Alexander the Great (323) to the Roman domination of Greece (146), when Hellenic culture expanded beyond the confines of Greece, and capital, money and technology were applied to warfare without ethical sanction.

HELOTS. Indentured serfs at Sparta, whose constant work allowed the Spartans to train continually and field a professional army of hoplites that did not have to farm.

HIPPEIS. 'Horsemen' whose mounted military service usually reflected their élite status in the political hierarchy of the Classical city state.

HOMERIC. The world of Homer's *Iliad* and *Odyssey*, whose values, practices and material conditions are drawn from some five centuries of oral transmission. Increasingly, however, scholars see the practices of the nascent city state in the poems, albeit with deliberate archaizing and epic grandeur.

HOPLITE. A heavy-armed infantry-man of the city state, who fought with his peers in the close formation of the phalanx. Protected with heavy metal helmet, breastplate, greaves and a wooden round shield, and armed with thrusting spear and short sword, the gear (*hopla*) probably gave the hoplite his name, and rendered him when in formation invincible from both light-armed and cavalry attack.

LACONIA. A southern peninsular region of the Peloponnese, controlled by its chief city at Sparta and seen as indistinguishable from Spartan culture.

LAWAGETAS. A Mycenaean military commander in charge of the armed forces of the palace.

LIGHT-ARMED. Poorer soldiers who could not afford full body armour. After the fifth century, they became more prominent than mere skirmishers, and all armies sought to hire them as mercenaries to meet new enemies and theatres of battle.

MACEDONIAN. Refers to the political unity established by Philip II from the various monarchies of northern Greece. Macedonians were generally felt by the city states to be quasi-Greeks: their lack of *polis* institutions, a nearly incompressible Greek dialect, and the legacy of kingship were seen as either anachronistic or foreign to the history and spirit of Hellenism.

MYCENAEAN. A late Bronze Age (1600–1200), Greek-speaking culture that developed on the mainland and Crete, characterized by prominent citadels and centralized bureaucracies such as those at Mycenae, Tiryns and Pylos.

PANHELLENIC. Literally 'all Greek', the desire and ideal to create a political homogeneity from the cultural and ethnic bonds of the various city states; usually realized only during festivals and athletic contests at shared sanctuaries.

PANOPLY. Usually refers to the hoplite infantryman's defensive and offensive ensemble, including helmet, shield, greaves, breastplate, spear and sword.

PELOPONNESE. A peninsula forming the southwestern part of Greece, mostly inhabited by Dorian states, which were in constant alliance with or in opposition to Sparta.

PELTAST. Light-armed skirmisher with small shield, often crescent-shaped (*peltê*), and armed with either javelin or spear, originally from Thrace but increasingly recruited from the poor and needy throughout Greece.

PHALANGITE. A hired pikemen in the phalanx of the Hellenistic age, who wore little armour, but wielded an enormous *sarissa*.

PHALANX. A column of heavily armed spearmen with neat ranks and files, designed to obliterate enemy infantrymen through the collision and push of shock battle, usually immune from the charges of horsemen. Used as a technical term in association with Classical Greek hoplites or Macedonian phalangites, who ranged from eight to fifty shields in depth.

POLIS. Often translated as city state, the term refers to an autonomous political community of Greeks. The *polis* comprised a central urban centre surrounded by farms and grazing land, inhabited by free citizens who followed constitutional law and fought on the approval of the assembly.

PROMACHOI. Greek for 'fighters in the front', a prestigious term used from Homer to the Hellenistic age for those who battled at the front of the phalanx.

SARISSA. A Macedonian pike, ranging from 14 to 20 feet in length, usually of cornel wood with a heavy iron tip and bronze butt-spike.

SIMILARS. The élite minority of adult male citizens at Sparta – hoplites whose egalitarianism extended from military to private life; often known as Spartiates, Peers or Equals.

TRIREME. A sleek, fast warship of the Classical Period, characterized by a crew of nearly 200 sailors, three banks of oars, and a large wooden and bronze ram.

WANAX. A Mycenaean lord, who probably held supreme power and managed the affairs of the palace and surrounding land.

WESTERN. A cultural tradition that originated in Europe, in and to the west of Greece, but which soon evolved beyond both criteria of race and region, to define a set of values and practices – chief among them being consensual government, capitalism, individual rights, civil liberties, separation of state and religion, and unfettered inquiry and expression.

ZEUGITAI. Those who met a property qualification – most notably at Athens – entitling them to political rights and infantry service in the early *polis*. The *zeugitai* were originally middling agrarians, often synonymous with those who owned their own armour and fought as hoplites in the early phalanx.

Notable Greeks at war

Aeneas Tacticus, an Arcadian general (367), wrote the earliest surviving Greek military treatise, a work on siegecraft, which is a rich source of Greek stratagems to protect cities against attack.

Aeschylus (525–456), the great Athenian tragedian, author of the Oresteia and some ninety other tragedies (seven alone survive), fought at Marathon, where his brother was killed on the beach. His epitaph records only his military service.

Agesilaus (445–359), as Spartan king for nearly forty years campaigned in Asia, Egypt, and on the Greek mainland to extend Spartan hegemony – a mostly failed enterprise since the king had no real understanding of the role of finance, fleets or siegecraft in a new era of war.

Alcibiades (451–404),the flamboyant Athenian politician and general, at one time or another was in the service of Athens, Sparta and Persia. As architect of the disastrous Sicilian expedition, and advocate of the Spartan occupation of Decelea, he helped to ruin the power of fifth-century Athens.

Alexander the Great (356–323), through sheer military genius conquered the Persian empire in little more than a decade. But Alexander's megalomania and desire for divine honours helped to pervert the legacy of Hellenism and left hundreds of thousands of Asians dead and displaced in his murderous wake. Ancient and modern ethical assessments of Alexander vary widely and depend entirely on the particular value one places on military prodigy and conquest.

Antigonus (382–301), one of the more gifted of Alexander's generals, spent his later years trying to consolidate Alexander's empire under a single dynasty. His plans were at once realized and crushed at Ipsus where he died in battle at the age of 81.

Aristides (d. 467), nicknamed 'the Just', proved to be an able Athenian statesman. Aristides shared command at the battles of Marathon, Salamis and Plataea and helped to lay the foundations of the Athenian empire.

Brasidas (d. 422), was without question the most innovative commander in the history of the Spartan state. By using light-armed troops and freed helots to carve out Spartan bases and win allies, his efforts checked Athenian ambitions for much of the early Peloponnesian war, until his death at Amphipolis.

Chabrias (420–357) fought on behalf of Athens for over three decades, as professional commander at various times against Persia, Sparta and Boeotia. He was adept at using light-armed troops in concert with fortifications and as mobile marines.

Cleon (d. 422) appears as a roguish demagogue in Thucydides' history, but he was not always inept in the field, and won an impressive victory over the Spartans at Pylos (425) before dying in the battle for Amphipolis.

Demosthenes (d. 413), an active Athenian general of the Peloponnesian war; his successes at Pylos and Amphilochia were more than offset by crushing defeats in Aetolia, Boeotia, Megara – and Sicily.

Demosthenes (384–322), as the greatest Athenian orator and champion of Greek freedom, devoted his life to crafting an alliance of Greek states against Philip of Macedon. When his plans finally materialized at Chaeronea, the Greeks were demolished and Demosthenes ran home to organize the defenses of Athens.

Epaminondas (d. 362), the talented Theban general and statesman, accomplished the destruction of Spartan apartheid and won a crushing victory over the Spartan phalanx at Leuctra. The Theban hegemony essentially ended with his death at Mantinea.

Iphicrates (415–353) brought light-armed peltasts to the fore of Greek warfare of the fourth century. As an Athenian general, he destroyed a regiment of Spartan hoplites at Corinth and employed his military innovations in various campaigns on behalf of Athens.

Leonidas (reigned 490–480), as Spartan king led an allied Greek force to Thermopylae. His courage became mythical through his stubborn refusal to abandon the pass and his desire instead to die, with 299 of his royal guard, still fighting.

Lysander (d. 395), a Spartan general, who commanded the Peloponnesian fleet in its final victories over Athens in the Peloponnesian war. His attempt to extend Spartan hegemony to Asia Minor and Boeotia was cut short by his death in battle at Haliartus.

Miltiades (550–489) was largely responsible for the Greek victory at Marathon; a fatal infection from a battle wound on Paros ended his plans for early Athenian naval expansion in the Aegean.

Pagondas, the fifth-century Theban general at Delium (424) whose innovative use of reserves, a deep phalanx and cavalry defeated the Athenians and marked a turning-point in the history of Greek battle tactics.

Parmenio (400–330), the gifted cavalry commander of Alexander, whose skilled efforts on the left wing of the Macedonian battle line ensured victory in the major battles against the Persians. He was executed by Alexander on unproven charges of conspiracy.

Pausanias (d. c. 470), the Spartan regent and general who commanded the Greeks at Plataea. Pausanias' hoplite proficiency was vital to the Greek cause, but his later mismanagement of the Greek alliance led to his eventual disgrace and death.

Pelopidas (d. 364), the Theban general (and close associate of Epaminondas), who commanded the Sacred Band at Leuctra. He played a notable role in a series of Theban victories until he was killed at Cynoscephalae.

Pericles (495–429), the brilliant Athenian imperialist and statesman who for nearly thirty years oversaw the rise of Athenian economic, military and political power. He died at the beginning of the Peloponnesian war from the plague – a result of his own policy of forced evacuation of Attica within the confines of Athens.

Philip II (382–336), the brilliant and ruthless architect of Macedonian hegemony, who conquered Greece through political realism, tactical innovation and strategic brilliance. Had he not been assassinated, the Macedonian army might have been content with the conquest of western Persia.

Plato (429–347), the great Athenian philosopher whose devotion to Socrates, and involvement in the politics of Sicily, left him with keen interests in war and the state, ranging from the tactical and strategic to the cultural and political.

Ptolemy I (367–282), a veteran lieutenant of Alexander, who, on the latter's death, claimed Egypt as his imperial province. He was the most astute of all Alexander's successors, and lived to found the Ptolemaic dynasty in Egypt and write a memoir of Alexander's campaigns.

Pyrrhus (319–272), the brilliant Epirote general, whose invasion of Italy became proverbial as profligate – a costly tactical victory without long-term strategic success. He died ignominiously at Argos, hit by a roof tile in the street, and then decapitated.

Socrates (469–399), the hero of Plato's dialogues and founder of western philosophy, fought heroically at Potidaea, Amphipolis and Delium. He stood courageously against both the democratic mob and tyrannical revolutionists in their illegal efforts to execute those accused.

Sophocles (496–406), the great Athenian playwright, was a general at the Athenian conquest of Samos and served on the Athenian board of audit after the disaster on Sicily. His dramatic career paralleled the high tide of Athenian imperialism.

Themistocles (524–459), the gifted Athenian general and architect of Athenian naval supremacy, was responsible for the creation of a 200-ship Athenian navy and its brilliant conduct at Salamis. His later years were characterized by political intrigue and condemnation by both Athens and Sparta.

Thucydides (460?–395?), the brilliant historian of the Peloponnesian war, saw battle first hand as the Athenian admiral at Amphipolis; for his relative failure there he was exiled for twenty years by the Athenian Assembly. Thucydides' history reflects a veteran's intimate knowledge of tactical manoeuvre and strategic thinking, and the interplay between military operations and civilian audit and control.

Xenophon (428–354), Greek historian and antiquarian; his extant work on everything from military history to biography and military science reflects his long and difficult career as an Athenian exile, intimate of Socrates, veteran of the Ten Thousand, and close associate of the Spartan high military command.

Further Reading

THERE ARE GENERAL CHAPTERS for the non-specialist on fighting of the ancient Near East, Egyptians and the Mycenaeans in A. Ferrill's *The Origins of War* (New York, 1985). The best recent survey of late Bronze Age battle is Robert Drews' *The End of the Bronze Age. Changes in Warfare and the Catastrophe c. 1200 BC* (Princeton, 1993). H. van Wees' *Status Warriors. Violence and Society in Homer and History* (Amsterdam, 1992) is a valuable and original review of Homeric battle descriptions.

The field of Greek military history has exploded in the last twenty years, as a result of continuing publication of W. K. Pritchett's vast work of some twenty-five years of ceaseless devotion, *The Greek State at War*, Parts I–V (Berkeley 1971–91), and his accompanying eight volumes, *Studies in Ancient Greek Topography* (Berkeley 1965–89; Amsterdam, 1991–3), which deal with battlefields and campaign routes in Greece. Early Greek warfare before the fifth century is the subject of P. Greenhalgh's sober *Early Greek Warfare: Horsemen and Chariots in the Homeric and Archaic Ages* (Cambridge, UK, 1973); the rise of hoplites is tied to the emergence of a new agrarian class and ideology in V. D. Hanson's *The Other Greeks. The Agrarian Roots of Western Civilization* (New York, 1995).

Reliable and quite readable are the accounts on tactics, strategy, and the evolution of hoplite war in F. Adcock, *The Greek and Macedonian Art of War* (Berkeley, 1957), P. Ducrey, *Warfare in Ancient Greece* (New York, 1986), Y. Garlan, *War in the Ancient World* (New York, 1975), and especially J. K. Anderson, *Military Theory and Practice in the Age of Xenophon* (Berkeley, 1970). Some interesting artistic re-creations of Greek warfare, as well as valuable maps and charts, are found in the surveys of J. Hackett (ed.), *A History of War in the Ancient World* (London, 1989), J. Warry, *Warfare in the Classical World* (New York, 1980), and P. Connolly, *Greece and Rome at War* (London, 1981). There is now a brief sourcebook of ancient passages on Greek warfare in M. Sage (ed.), *Warfare in Ancient Greece* (London, 1996).

The environment and experience of hoplite fighting are covered by V. D. Hanson, *The Western Way of War. Infantry Battle in Classical Greece* (New York, 1989), and in a collection of essays by nine military historians, V. D. Hanson (ed.), *Hoplites: The Ancient Greek Battle Experience* (London, 1991). See also the excellent articles in A. B. Lloyd (ed.), *Battle in Antiquity* (London, 1996). Social and economic problems of Greek warfare concern V. D. Hanson, *Warfare and Agriculture in Classical Greece* (Pisa, 1983; 2nd ed. Berkeley, 1998), and J. Rich and G. Shipley (eds.), *War and Society in the Greek World* (London, 1993). Doyne Dawson, *The Origins of Western Warfare. Militarism and Morality in the Ancient Greek World* (Boulder, 1996), has a fine synopsis of the philosophical assumptions of the Greeks concerning war.

The study of Greek arms and armour rests still on the work of A. Snodgrass, *Early Greek Armour and Weapons* (Edinburgh, 1964) and *Arms and Armour of the Greeks* (Ithaca, NY, 1967), now updated by E. Jarva's curious but original *Archaiologica on Archaic Greek Body Armour* (Rovaniemi, Finland, 1995). There are excellent studies on the regionalism and specialization in Greek warfare; see especially, J. Lazenby, *The Spartan Army* (Westminster, UK, 1985), and J. Best, *Thracian Peltasts and their Influence on Greek Warfare* (Groningen, 1969). For ancient cavalry, now see the trio of G. Bugh, *The Horsemen of Athens* (Princeton, 1988), L. Worley, *Hippeis. The Cavalry of Ancient Greece* (Boulder, 1994), and I. G. Spence, *The Cavalry of Classical Greece. A Social and Military History with Particular Reference to Athens* (Oxford, 1993).

A comprehensive catalogue of Greek battles in English is desperately needed to update J. Kromayer and G. Veith, *Antike Schlachtfelder* (Berlin, 1903–31). D. Kagan's four-volume *New History of the Peloponnesian War* (Ithaca, NY, 1969–87) has brief, though fine, accounts of the major land and sea battles between 431 and 404. R. Gabriel and D. Boose Jr. have very general accounts of a few Greek battles in *The Great Battles of Antiquity* (Westport, Conn., 1994).

No comprehensive survey exists for the long and complicated story of Hellenistic warfare, but the general outlines can be pieced together through

Here a craftsman cuts away imperfections from a recently cast Corinthian bronze hoplite helmet. Armour fabrication is a favourite theme of the classical vase-painters, who were not only aware of the centrality of military equipment in Greek life, but also sensitive to the artistic beauty of the hoplite panoply itself. A fully armoured phalanx on the move, like a trireme with oars in motion, was not merely an instrument of death, but a terrifyingly beautiful object in its own right.

a variety of excellent, though specialized studies. A dated, but still valuable overview are W. W. Tarn's lectures, *Hellenistic Military and Naval Developments* (Cambridge, UK, 1930). More detailed is the introductory volume of H. Delbrück, *Warfare in Antiquity* (Westport, Conn., 1975).

Too numerous to list are the scores of biographies of Alexander the Great that discuss his military record in detail. N. G. L. Hammond's *Alexander the Great: King, Commander, and Statesman* (London, 1981) reveals the author's lifetime mastery of Greek military history. Still useful is J. F. C. Fuller's, *The Generalship of Alexander the Great* (London, 1960). For Alexander's army on the move, cf. D. Engels, *Alexander the Great and the Logistics of the Macedonian Army* (Berkeley, 1978). An honest appraisal of Alexander is best found in A. B. Bosworth, *Conquest and Empire. The Reign of Alexander the Great* (Cambridge, 1988).

The growing fourth-century and Hellenistic practice of hiring armies is the subject of G. T. Griffith's *Mercenaries of the Hellenistic World* (Cambridge, UK, 1935), and H. W. Parke's *Greek Mercenary Soldiers* (Oxford, 1933). It is sometimes forgotten that P. Cartledge's *Agesilaos and the Crisis of Sparta* (Baltimore, 1987) contains the best synopsis of fourth-century Greek warfare. Fortifications and the massive walls of Hellenistic cities are covered well by A. W. Lawrence, *Greek Aims in Fortification* (Oxford, 1979), F. E. Winter, *Greek Fortifications* (Toronto, 1971), and J. Ober, *Fortress Attica. Defense of the Athenian Land Frontier. 404–322* (Leiden, 1985). F. W. Marsden reviews the evolution of catapults and siegecraft in his two-volume *Greek and Roman Artillery* (Oxford, 1969–71). H. H. Scullard, *The Elephant in the Greek and Roman World* (Ithaca, NY, 1974), is primarily concerned with military applications of elephants in the battles between Greeks and Romans. B. Bar-Kochava, *The Seleucid Army* (Cambridge, UK, 1976), is the sole specialized account devoted to the armies of the Successors. Both E. L. Wheeler, *Stratagem and the Vocabulary of Military Trickery* (Leiden, 1988), and D. Whitehead, *Aineias the Tactician: How to Survive Under Siege* (Oxford, 1990), discuss the growing genre of Greek military science and contemplation.

In general what is now needed is a comprehensive – tactics, topography and source criticism – and systematic catalogue of the major Greek battles from Marathon to Pydna. In addition, a strictly military history of the Peloponnesian war is long overdue, as is an account of the Theban army. No single-volume, comprehensive work exists on Hellenistic warfare. A military prosopography that might catalogue the battle service of all major Greek figures would be useful, as well as a strictly economic analysis of the costs of Classical and Hellenistic fighting.

Statistics

PERFORMANCE CHARACTERISTICS OF ANCIENT WEAPONS

Weapon	Weight in pounds	Speed in feet per second	Impact area in inches	Area of wound in inches	Impact energy in foot-pounds
Stone mace	1.8	60	3.0	9.0	101.3
Gladius (hacking)	1.8	60	1.5	4.0	101.0
Penetrating axe	2.2	48	0.5	1.75	77.5
Sickle sword	1.8	53	4.0	6.5	77.5
Spear (overhand)	1.5	55	1/32	3.6	70.8
Cutting axe	2.0	48	2.5	5.0	70.5
Eye axe	2.0	48	0.75	2.25	70.5
Javelin	1.3	58	1/32	2.6	67.1
Arrow	553 grains	197	1/32	2.0	47.4
Gladius (thrust)	1.8	28	1/32	4.7	21.3
Sling	500 grains	120	0.75	1.2	16.0
Spear (underhand)	1.5	24	1/32	3.6	13.5

(From R. Gabriel and K. Metz, *From Sumer to Rome* (Westport, CT, 1991), 59

DEATH RATES IN CLASSICAL AND HELLENISTIC BATTLES

Battle	Winners	Losers	Winners killed	Losers killed
Marathon 490 bc	10,000 Athenians	30,000 Persians	192 (2%)	6,400 (21%)
Delium 424 bc	18,500 Boeotians	c. 10,000 Athenians	500 (2.7%)	1,000+ (10%)
Gaugamela 331 bc	50,000 Macedonians	c. 250,000 Persians	c. 500 (1%)	50,000+ (20%)
Pydna 168 bc	30,000 Romans	c. 44,000 Macedonians	statistically unimportant	20,000 (45.4%)

THE COST OF RUNNING A WAR

1 drachma = about a day's wage in the fifth century

EXPENSES

To send 40,000 men from Athens to Sicily for a two-year campaign	20,500,00 drs
To conduct the Athenian military for a year during the Peloponnesian War	12,000,000 drs
To conduct a large siege for a year	5–8,000,000 drs
To man 100 triremes for a month (pay and supplies)	1,400,000 drs
To field an army of 10,000 hoplites for a week	70,000 drs
To field 1,000 horsemen for a week	14,000 drs

CAPITAL OUTLAY FOR WEAPONS AND EQUIPMENT

The cost of building a fortification circuit wall of 4 miles	1,500,000 drs
The cost of building/outfitting a single trireme	10–12,000 drs
The cost of a good war horse	500–6,000 drs
The cost of a hoplite's panoply	100–300 drs

COMPARATIVE NON-MILITARY EXPENDITURES

The cost of building the Parthenon	5,000,000 drs
The cost of putting on a Sophoclean play	1,500–3,000 drs
The cost of a slave	300–500 drs

RESOURCES OF THE MAJOR GREEK BELLIGERENTS AT THE OUTBREAK OF THE PELOPONNESIAN WAR

AVAILABLE BATTLE-READY HOPLITES

Athens/ Attica	13,000
Athenian allies	10,000
TOTAL	**23,000**

Thebes/Boeotian Confederacy	10–12,000
Sparta/Laconia	8–10,000
Peloponnesian allies	20,000
TOTAL	**40,000**

NUMBER OF TRIREMES

Athens/ Attica	300
Athenian allies	100
TOTAL	**400**

Thebes/Boeotian Confederacy	0
Sparta/Laconia	0
Peloponnesian allies	100
TOTAL	**100**

CITIZEN POPULATION (ADULT MALES, FREE WOMEN AND CHILDREN)

Athens/ Attica	150,000
Thebes/Boeotian Confederacy	100,000
Sparta/Laconia	40,000

SIZE OF TERRITORY

Athens/ Attica	c. 1,000 sq. miles	(2,590 sq.km)
Thebes/Boeotia	c. 1,000 sq. miles	(2,590 sq.km)
Sparta/Laconia	c. 2,000 sq. miles	(5,180 sq.km)

NUMBER OF SLAVES

Athens/Attica	100,000
Thebes/Boeotia	10,000
Sparta/Laconia	250,000 helots in Messenia and Laconia

Index

Picture credits

Every effort has been made to contact the copyright holders for images reproduced in this book. The publishers would welcome any errors or omissions being brought to their attention.

The Art Archive pp. 2, 29, 46, 55, 127; Bridgeman Art Library pp. 6, 12, 14, 15, 17, 18, 63, 101, 113, 116, 121, 134, 138, 162, 172; Sonia Halliday Photographs pp. 20, 28, 30, 37, 42, 84, 142, 164, 170, 204; Peter Newark Pictures pp. 40, 45, 50, 57, 85, 106, 137, 190, 194; Mary Evans Picture Library pp. 48, 90; Victor Davis Hanson pp. 152, 156–7.

The drawings on pp. 27, 28, 58, 59, 60, 158, 161 and 200 are by Peter Smith and Malcolm Swanston of Arcadia Editions Ltd.